# Clean Eating Cookbook:

*Beginner-Friendly Guide with 200+ Quick & Nourishing Recipes to Enhance Energy Levels, Strengthen Immunity, and Enjoy a Healthier Life with Wholesome Foods Daily*

Jillian Nunez

© 2025 Jillian Nunez. All rights reserved.

No part of this product may be duplicated, saved, or transmitted in any form, digital, print, or electronic, without the publisher's prior written consent, with the exception of small extracts used in reviews or instructional content. This cookbook is meant for personal use only. Redistribution or resale, in whole or in part, is prohibited without explicit consent.

**Disclaimer**

This cookbook is only for informative purposes only. It includes dishes that follow clean eating concepts, focusing on simple, minimally processed products.

It is not meant to provide medical or dietary advice. Clean eating can be interpreted differently and may not fulfill the specific demands of each individual. If you have food allergies, medical issues, or special dietary needs, speak with a trained healthcare provider or registered dietitian before making significant dietary adjustments.

The author and publisher accept no responsibility for any positive or bad health effects that occur from the use of this content.

# TABLE OF CONTENTS

- **INTRODUCTION** .................................................................................................................. 9
- **BREAKFASTS & SMOOTHIES** ........................................................................................ 11
  - ALMOND BUTTER & BANANA OVERNIGHT OATS ............................................................ 12
  - CHIA PUDDING WITH BERRIES & COCONUT ................................................................... 12
  - QUINOA BREAKFAST BOWL WITH ALMONDS & HONEY ................................................ 13
  - GREEN DETOX SMOOTHIE WITH SPINACH & AVOCADO ............................................... 13
  - TURMERIC & GINGER ANTI-INFLAMMATORY SMOOTHIE ............................................. 14
  - FLUFFY OAT & BANANA PANCAKES .................................................................................. 14
  - SWEET POTATO & CINNAMON BREAKFAST HASH .......................................................... 15
  - PROTEIN-PACKED GREEK YOGURT PARFAIT ................................................................... 15
  - APPLE CINNAMON BAKED OATMEAL ................................................................................ 16
  - SUPERFOOD ACAI SMOOTHIE BOWL ................................................................................. 16
  - BLUEBERRY & ALMOND BUTTER SMOOTHIE .................................................................. 17
  - COCONUT & PINEAPPLE TROPICAL SMOOTHIE .............................................................. 17
  - VANILLA CHIA PUDDING WITH MANGO ........................................................................... 18
  - HOMEMADE BUCKWHEAT GRANOLA WITH NUTS ......................................................... 18
  - CARROT CAKE OVERNIGHT OATS ...................................................................................... 19
  - STRAWBERRY & COCONUT CHIA PUDDING .................................................................... 19
  - PEANUT BUTTER & CACAO POWER SMOOTHIE .............................................................. 20
  - SPICED QUINOA PORRIDGE WITH APPLES ....................................................................... 20
  - GREEN APPLE & KALE SMOOTHIE ..................................................................................... 21
  - GOLDEN MILK TURMERIC SMOOTHIE .............................................................................. 21
  - MATCHA ENERGY BOOSTING SMOOTHIE ........................................................................ 22
  - AVOCADO & BERRY BREAKFAST TOAST .......................................................................... 22
  - CHOCOLATE ALMOND BUTTER PROTEIN SHAKE ........................................................... 23
  - CREAMY OATMEAL WITH FLAXSEEDS & WALNUTS ...................................................... 23
  - DATE & NUT SUPERFOOD BREAKFAST BARS .................................................................. 24
  - LEMON BLUEBERRY PROTEIN PANCAKES ....................................................................... 24
- **SNACKS & ENERGY BITES** ............................................................................................. 25
  - NO-BAKE ALMOND & DATE ENERGY BALLS .................................................................... 26
  - SPICED CHICKPEA CRUNCHIES .......................................................................................... 26
  - SUPERFOOD TRAIL MIX WITH CACAO NIBS ..................................................................... 27
  - HOMEMADE FLAXSEED CRACKERS .................................................................................. 27
  - ROASTED CINNAMON ALMONDS ....................................................................................... 28
  - CHIA SEED PROTEIN BARS .................................................................................................. 28
  - APPLE SLICES WITH ALMOND BUTTER & CINNAMON ................................................... 29

- CARROT & HUMMUS WRAPS .................................................................................................. 29
- OVEN-BAKED KALE CHIPS .................................................................................................... 30
- QUINOA & PEANUT BUTTER ENERGY BITES ..................................................................... 30
- CRUNCHY ROASTED PUMPKIN SEEDS ................................................................................ 31
- DARK CHOCOLATE & WALNUT BITES .................................................................................. 31
- AVOCADO & TOMATO RICE CAKES ..................................................................................... 32
- COCONUT & CASHEW BLISS BALLS .................................................................................... 32
- NO-SUGAR APPLE CHIPS ....................................................................................................... 33
- CUCUMBER & HUMMUS ROLL-UPS ..................................................................................... 33
- PROTEIN-PACKED CHIA CRACKERS ................................................................................... 34
- SPICY EDAMAME SNACK BITES ........................................................................................... 34
- BANANA & ALMOND BUTTER RICE CAKES ........................................................................ 35
- ROASTED SWEET POTATO WEDGES WITH PAPRIKA ..................................................... 35
- CRANBERRY & OAT GRANOLA BITES ................................................................................. 36
- CARROT & ZUCCHINI MUFFINS ............................................................................................. 36
- TURMERIC-SPICED MIXED NUTS ......................................................................................... 37
- STRAWBERRY & COCONUT YOGURT BARK ..................................................................... 37
- HEMP SEED & HONEY PROTEIN BARS ............................................................................... 38
- CHEWY FIG & NUT SNACK BARS .......................................................................................... 38

## SALADS & DRESSINGS ............................................................................................................... 39

- QUINOA & AVOCADO DETOX SALAD .................................................................................. 40
- KALE & ROASTED CHICKPEA SALAD .................................................................................. 40
- MANGO & BLACK BEAN SUMMER SALAD ......................................................................... 41
- MEDITERRANEAN CUCUMBER & TOMATO SALAD ......................................................... 41
- SPINACH & POMEGRANATE SUPERFOOD SALAD .......................................................... 42
- ASIAN SESAME GINGER SLAW ............................................................................................. 42
- ROASTED BEET & WALNUT SALAD ..................................................................................... 43
- LEMON GARLIC LENTIL SALAD ............................................................................................ 43
- GRILLED CHICKEN & AVOCADO BOWL .............................................................................. 44
- APPLE & WALNUT ARUGULA SALAD ................................................................................... 44
- ZESTY QUINOA & CRANBERRY SALAD .............................................................................. 45
- RAINBOW VEGGIE NOODLE SALAD .................................................................................... 45
- AVOCADO & ROASTED SWEET POTATO SALAD ............................................................. 46
- CLASSIC GREEK SALAD WITH A TWIST ............................................................................. 46
- CABBAGE & CARROT DETOX SALAD ................................................................................. 47
- TURMERIC & GINGER DRESSING ........................................................................................ 47
- HOMEMADE HONEY MUSTARD DRESSING ...................................................................... 48
- CILANTRO LIME VINAIGRETTE .............................................................................................. 48

- CREAMY TAHINI DRESSING ... 49
- MAPLE BALSAMIC DRESSING ... 49
- SPICY MANGO DRESSING ... 50
- VEGAN RANCH DRESSING ... 50
- GARLIC & LEMON YOGURT DRESSING ... 51
- ROASTED RED PEPPER DRESSING ... 51
- RASPBERRY VINAIGRETTE ... 52
- GINGER MISO DRESSING ... 52

**SOUPS & STEWS ... 53**
- CARROT GINGER DETOX SOUP ... 54
- ROASTED TOMATO & BASIL SOUP ... 54
- SWEET POTATO & COCONUT SOUP ... 55
- BUTTERNUT SQUASH & APPLE SOUP ... 55
- SPICED LENTIL & KALE SOUP ... 56
- QUINOA & VEGETABLE BROTH BOWL ... 56
- CREAMY CAULIFLOWER & GARLIC SOUP ... 57
- TURMERIC & LEMON CHICKPEA SOUP ... 57
- HEARTY MUSHROOM & BARLEY STEW ... 58
- MOROCCAN SPICED CARROT SOUP ... 58
- ROASTED RED PEPPER & QUINOA SOUP ... 59
- THAI-INSPIRED COCONUT CURRY SOUP ... 59
- MEDITERRANEAN LENTIL SOUP ... 60
- GREEN PEA & MINT SOUP ... 60
- DETOX CABBAGE SOUP ... 61
- BLACK BEAN & SWEET POTATO STEW ... 61
- GINGER & TURMERIC IMMUNE BOOST SOUP ... 62
- PUMPKIN & WHITE BEAN SOUP ... 62
- CHICKPEA & SPINACH STEW ... 63
- SAVORY ROASTED GARLIC SOUP ... 63
- ZUCCHINI & BASIL CREAM SOUP ... 64
- MUSHROOM & WILD RICE SOUP ... 64
- TOMATO & ROASTED RED PEPPER STEW ... 65
- KALE & WHITE BEAN SOUP ... 65
- SPICY CAULIFLOWER SOUP ... 66
- LEMON & PARSNIP SOUP ... 66

**MAIN DISHES ... 67**
- GRILLED LEMON HERB CHICKEN ... 68
- BAKED SALMON WITH GARLIC & DILL ... 68

STUFFED BELL PEPPERS WITH QUINOA & BLACK BEANS ................................................................. 69

CHICKPEA & SWEET POTATO BUDDHA BOWL ................................................................................. 69

ZUCCHINI NOODLES WITH PESTO ....................................................................................................... 70

LENTIL & VEGETABLE STIR-FRY ............................................................................................................ 70

GARLIC & HERB ROASTED TOFU .......................................................................................................... 71

MEDITERRANEAN STUFFED EGGPLANT ............................................................................................... 71

BALSAMIC GLAZED CHICKEN BREAST ................................................................................................. 72

SPAGHETTI SQUASH & TOMATO SAUCE ............................................................................................. 72

TURMERIC ROASTED CAULIFLOWER STEAKS ..................................................................................... 73

AVOCADO & BLACK BEAN WRAPS ....................................................................................................... 73

HONEY MUSTARD BAKED TEMPEH ...................................................................................................... 74

QUINOA & KALE POWER BOWL ............................................................................................................ 74

THAI-INSPIRED TOFU CURRY ................................................................................................................ 75

SPINACH & CHICKPEA STIR-FRY .......................................................................................................... 75

SHEET PAN SALMON & VEGETABLES .................................................................................................. 76

GARLIC BUTTER SHRIMP WITH ZOODLES .......................................................................................... 76

SPICED TURKEY & VEGGIE SKILLET ..................................................................................................... 77

MOROCCAN CHICKPEA STEW ............................................................................................................... 77

LEMON DILL GRILLED CHICKEN ........................................................................................................... 78

MUSHROOM & LENTIL MEATBALLS ..................................................................................................... 78

VEGAN TOFU & BROCCOLI STIR-FRY .................................................................................................. 79

ROASTED ROOT VEGETABLE MEDLEY ................................................................................................. 79

COCONUT CURRY LENTILS .................................................................................................................... 80

HERB-CRUSTED WHITE FISH ................................................................................................................. 80

**SIDE DISHES & VEGETABLES ............................................................................................................... 81**

ROASTED BRUSSELS SPROUTS WITH BALSAMIC GLAZE .................................................................. 82

GARLIC MASHED CAULIFLOWER .......................................................................................................... 82

SPICY ROASTED SWEET POTATOES .................................................................................................... 83

LEMON & HERB QUINOA ....................................................................................................................... 83

GRILLED ASPARAGUS WITH LEMON ZEST .......................................................................................... 84

SAUTÉED GARLIC KALE .......................................................................................................................... 84

COCONUT GINGER CARROT FRIES ...................................................................................................... 85

ZUCCHINI & PARMESAN BAKE ............................................................................................................. 85

ROASTED BEET & ORANGE MEDLEY ................................................................................................... 86

TURMERIC-SPICED LENTILS .................................................................................................................. 86

HONEY ROASTED CARROTS .................................................................................................................. 87

CUMIN-SPICED CHICKPEAS ................................................................................................................... 87

QUINOA & HERB PILAF .......................................................................................................................... 88

- BALSAMIC ROASTED MUSHROOMS .................................................................................................. 88
- SPAGHETTI SQUASH WITH PESTO .................................................................................................... 89
- AVOCADO & TOMATO SALSA ............................................................................................................ 89
- SAUTÉED GREEN BEANS WITH ALMONDS ........................................................................................ 90
- CINNAMON ROASTED BUTTERNUT SQUASH .................................................................................. 90
- SWEET CORN & BLACK BEAN SALAD ................................................................................................ 91
- MISO GLAZED EGGPLANT .................................................................................................................. 91
- CARROT & GINGER SLAW .................................................................................................................. 92
- STEAMED BROCCOLI WITH GARLIC .................................................................................................. 92
- LEMON & HERB ROASTED CAULIFLOWER ....................................................................................... 93
- MANGO & CUCUMBER SALSA ........................................................................................................... 93
- DILL & LEMON CUCUMBER SALAD ................................................................................................... 94
- HERB-INFUSED BROWN RICE ............................................................................................................ 94

**HEALTHY DRINKS & TONICS .................................................................................................................. 95**

- TURMERIC & GINGER GOLDEN MILK ............................................................................................... 96
- MATCHA GREEN TEA LATTE .............................................................................................................. 96
- DETOX LEMON & CUCUMBER WATER ............................................................................................. 97
- BERRY ANTIOXIDANT SMOOTHIE ..................................................................................................... 97
- GINGER & HONEY IMMUNITY SHOT ................................................................................................ 98
- MINT & WATERMELON REFRESHER ................................................................................................. 98
- ALMOND CHAI SPICED TEA ............................................................................................................... 99
- CINNAMON-SPICED APPLE CIDER .................................................................................................... 99
- COCONUT WATER & LIME COOLER ................................................................................................ 100
- GREEN APPLE & SPINACH JUICE ..................................................................................................... 100
- HIBISCUS & ROSEHIP VITAMIN C TEA ............................................................................................ 101
- ALOE VERA & LEMON HYDRATION DRINK .................................................................................... 101
- GOLDEN TURMERIC DETOX TEA ..................................................................................................... 102
- COCONUT MATCHA ENERGY BOOST ............................................................................................. 102
- BLUEBERRY & ACAI ANTIOXIDANT SMOOTHIE ............................................................................. 103
- WARM LEMON & CAYENNE DETOX WATER .................................................................................. 103
- GINGER & PINEAPPLE DIGESTIVE TONIC ....................................................................................... 104
- HONEY-LAVENDER SLEEP TEA ........................................................................................................ 104
- CINNAMON & ALMOND SPICED LATTE ......................................................................................... 105
- FRESH WATERMELON & BASIL JUICE ............................................................................................. 105
- CARROT, ORANGE & GINGER WELLNESS JUICE ............................................................................ 106
- APPLE CIDER VINEGAR MORNING SHOT ....................................................................................... 106
- PEPPERMINT & LEMON HERBAL INFUSION ................................................................................... 107
- CUCUMBER & MINT COOLING TONIC ............................................................................................ 107

- ANTI-INFLAMMATORY GREEN JUICE ... 108
- POMEGRANATE & LIME SPARKLING DRINK ... 108

## DESSERTS & TREATS ... 109

- NO-BAKE ALMOND BUTTER BROWNIES ... 110
- CHIA SEED CHOCOLATE PUDDING ... 110
- COCONUT & DARK CHOCOLATE BLISS BALLS ... 111
- APPLE CINNAMON BAKED OAT BARS ... 111
- DATE & WALNUT ENERGY FUDGE ... 112
- RAW CASHEW CHEESECAKE BITES ... 112
- BANANA PEANUT BUTTER ICE CREAM ... 113
- LEMON COCONUT MACAROONS ... 113
- MAPLE & PECAN BAKED PEARS ... 114
- HOMEMADE RASPBERRY CHIA JAM ... 114
- DARK CHOCOLATE AVOCADO MOUSSE ... 115
- OATMEAL & BLUEBERRY MUFFINS ... 115
- SWEET POTATO & CACAO FUDGE ... 116
- RAW CARROT CAKE BITES ... 116
- BAKED APPLE & CINNAMON CRISP ... 117
- CHOCOLATE-DIPPED BANANA BITES ... 117
- STRAWBERRY COCONUT YOGURT BARK ... 118
- PUMPKIN SPICE ENERGY BALLS ... 118
- MANGO & COCONUT SORBET ... 119
- MATCHA & PISTACHIO PROTEIN BALLS ... 119
- HONEY & ALMOND BAKED PEACHES ... 120
- CACAO NIB & DATE BROWNIES ... 120
- HAZELNUT & FIG RAW BARS ... 121
- GINGER-SPICED BAKED APPLES ... 121
- CRANBERRY & WALNUT OAT COOKIES ... 122
- VANILLA & CHIA YOGURT PARFAITS ... 122

# Introduction

Clean eating is a practical, evidence-based approach to improving dietary quality by emphasizing whole, minimally processed foods and eliminating or reducing artificial additives, preservatives, and overly refined ingredients. It is not a trend or a restrictive diet but rather a structured way of eating that focuses on food quality, ingredient transparency, and consistent nutritional intake. Clean eating is built on the principle that meals should be composed of foods in or close to their natural state, offering the highest possible nutritional value with the fewest unnecessary additives.

This approach centers on ingredients that provide essential macro- and micronutrients — including fiber, protein, healthy fats, vitamins, and minerals — without the inclusion of added sugars, excess sodium, trans fats, or synthetic compounds. Whole vegetables, fruits, lean proteins, legumes, nuts, seeds, and complex carbohydrates are prioritized because they support energy metabolism, digestive function, and overall metabolic efficiency. These foods also help maintain stable blood glucose levels, reduce total caloric density without compromising satiety, and offer better control over portion size due to their nutrient concentration and slower digestive rate.

Clean eating discourages reliance on processed foods that contribute to dietary imbalances. Common offenders include packaged snacks, frozen entrees with long ingredient lists, refined grains stripped of their fiber and micronutrients, and sugary beverages. These products often contain emulsifiers, preservatives, flavor enhancers, and colorings that serve no nutritional purpose. Although safe in small amounts, excessive intake of such compounds over time may disrupt gut integrity, influence insulin response, or interfere with the body's regulatory systems. Clean eating replaces these items with foods that support the body's natural processes — improving efficiency in digestion, nutrient absorption, and energy utilization.

Equally important to ingredient choice is the method of food preparation. Clean cooking relies on techniques that enhance the natural profile of ingredients without introducing additional dietary stressors. Baking, steaming, roasting, sautéing with minimal oil, and pressure cooking are all compatible with clean eating, as they preserve nutritional integrity without introducing harmful byproducts associated with excessive heat or deep-frying. Salt and sugar are used sparingly, if at all, and seasoning is derived from herbs, spices, citrus, and vinegar rather than processed sauces or flavor mixes. This control over preparation ensures more predictable nutritional outcomes and allows for more precise dietary planning, particularly for individuals managing chronic health conditions.

Clean eating can be adapted to a wide range of dietary needs. For individuals managing high blood pressure, it supports sodium reduction and increases potassium intake through fresh produce. Those with high cholesterol benefit from the increase in fiber and reduction in saturated fat and trans fat. People with type 2 diabetes find improved glycemic control through the emphasis on complex carbohydrates and the elimination of simple sugars. For individuals focused on weight reduction or maintenance, clean eating supports energy balance by naturally reducing energy-dense, nutrient-poor foods while maintaining food volume and nutrient density. The high fiber content of a clean diet improves digestion, supports healthy gut microbiota, and contributes to better absorption of nutrients and more consistent appetite regulation.

The clean eating framework also supports better food planning, shopping habits, and home cooking routines. Because meals are built around whole ingredients, grocery choices become more straightforward and meal preparation more predictable. Batch cooking, portioning, and storing meals are simplified by the consistent use of raw materials and basic cooking methods. This reduces dependence on restaurant meals or convenience foods, making it easier to manage calorie intake, monitor macronutrient balance, and avoid hidden additives.

Clean eating is not based on rigid exclusion, and it does not require the elimination of entire food groups unless medically necessary. It can include lean meats, dairy, grains, and oils — as long as those foods are unprocessed or minimally processed and consumed in forms that contribute to overall dietary balance. The key is that each ingredient should serve a clear nutritional purpose and be free from unnecessary additives. This principle makes clean eating highly adaptable across different cultures, preferences, and dietary protocols, including Mediterranean, vegetarian, gluten-free, or low-inflammatory approaches.

May the following meals assist you in incorporating this organized and practical eating style into your daily routine. Whether your aim is more energy, better metabolic management, or long-term health maintenance, this strategy promotes genuine success by providing consistent, ingredient-driven meals that are nutritionally clear and sustainable on a daily basis.

Warm regards and happy cooking.

# Breakfasts & Smoothies

## ALMOND BUTTER & BANANA OVERNIGHT OATS

**Servings 2 | Prep: 10 min | Cook: 0 min**

Start your day with a wholesome and satisfying breakfast that combines the creamy richness of almond butter with the natural sweetness of bananas. These overnight oats are perfect for busy mornings, offering a nutritious and delicious start to your day.

### Equipment

Mason Jars, Mixing Bowl, Spoon

### Ingredients

- 1 cup old-fashioned oats
- 1 cup unsweetened almond milk
- 2 tbsp almond butter
- 1 banana, sliced
- 1 tbsp chia seeds
- 1 tsp honey (optional)
- 1/2 tsp vanilla extract
- 1/4 tsp cinnamon

### Directions

1. In a mixing bowl, combine oats, almond milk, almond butter, chia seeds, vanilla extract, and cinnamon. Stir well.
2. Divide the mixture evenly into two mason jars.
3. Top each jar with banana slices and drizzle with honey if desired.
4. Seal the jars and refrigerate overnight, or for at least 4 hours.
5. In the morning, give the oats a good stir and enjoy directly from the jar or transfer to a bowl.

### Nutritional Information

Calories: 320, Protein: 8g, Carbohydrates: 45g, Fat: 12g, Fiber: 8g, Cholesterol: 0mg, Sodium: 60mg, Potassium: 450mg

## CHIA PUDDING WITH BERRIES & COCONUT

**Servings 4 | Prep: 10 min | Cook: 0 min**

A creamy, nutrient-packed breakfast or snack that combines the richness of coconut with the freshness of berries, perfect for a clean eating lifestyle.

### Equipment

Mixing Bowl, Whisk, Measuring Cups, Refrigerator

### Ingredients

- 1 cup unsweetened coconut milk
- 1/4 cup chia seeds
- 2 tbsp maple syrup
- 1 tsp vanilla extract
- 1 cup mixed berries (such as strawberries, blueberries, and raspberries)
- 1/4 cup unsweetened shredded coconut

### Directions

1. In a mixing bowl, whisk together the coconut milk, chia seeds, maple syrup, and vanilla extract until well combined.
2. Cover the bowl and refrigerate for at least 4 hours or overnight, allowing the chia seeds to absorb the liquid and thicken.
3. Once set, stir the chia pudding to ensure even consistency.
4. Divide the pudding into four serving bowls or jars.
5. Top each serving with mixed berries and a sprinkle of shredded coconut before serving.

### Nutritional Information

Calories: 180, Protein: 3g, Carbohydrates: 20g, Fat: 10g, Fiber: 7g, Cholesterol: 0mg, Sodium: 20mg, Potassium: 150mg

## QUINOA BREAKFAST BOWL WITH ALMONDS & HONEY

**Servings 2 | Prep: 5 min | Cook: 15 min**

A nourishing and hearty breakfast bowl that combines the nutty flavor of quinoa with the sweetness of honey and the crunch of almonds, perfect for a clean start to your day.

### Equipment

Medium Saucepan, Mixing Bowl, Spoon

### Ingredients

- 1 cup quinoa, rinsed
- 2 cups water
- 1/4 cup almonds, sliced
- 2 tbsp honey
- 1/2 cup fresh berries (e.g., blueberries, strawberries)
- 1/4 tsp cinnamon
- Pinch of salt

### Directions

1. In a medium saucepan, combine quinoa and water. Bring to a boil over medium-high heat.
2. Reduce heat to low, cover, and simmer for 15 minutes or until quinoa is tender and water is absorbed.
3. Fluff the quinoa with a fork and stir in the cinnamon and a pinch of salt.
4. Divide the quinoa into two bowls. Top each with sliced almonds, fresh berries, and a drizzle of honey.
5. Serve warm and enjoy your wholesome breakfast bowl.

### Nutritional Information

Calories: 320, Protein: 8g, Carbohydrates: 58g, Fat: 9g, Fiber: 6g, Cholesterol: 0mg, Sodium: 10mg, Potassium: 380mg

## GREEN DETOX SMOOTHIE WITH SPINACH & AVOCADO

**Servings 2 | Prep: 5 min | Cook: 0 min**

This vibrant green detox smoothie is a refreshing blend of nutrient-rich spinach and creamy avocado, perfect for a healthy start to your day.

### Equipment

Blender, Measuring Cups, Measuring Spoons

### Ingredients

- 2 cups fresh spinach
- 1 ripe avocado, peeled and pitted
- 1 cup unsweetened almond milk
- 1 tablespoon fresh lemon juice
- 1 teaspoon honey (optional)
- 1/2 cup ice cubes

### Directions

1. Add the fresh spinach and ripe avocado to the blender.
2. Pour in the unsweetened almond milk and fresh lemon juice.
3. Add honey for a touch of sweetness, if desired.
4. Top with ice cubes to chill the smoothie.
5. Blend on high until smooth and creamy.
6. Pour into glasses and serve immediately.

### Nutritional Information

Calories: 180, Protein: 4g, Carbohydrates: 18g, Fat: 12g, Fiber: 7g, Cholesterol: 0mg, Sodium: 60mg, Potassium: 600mg

# TURMERIC & GINGER ANTI-INFLAMMATORY SMOOTHIE

**Servings 2 | Prep: 5 min | Cook: 0 min**

This vibrant smoothie is a powerhouse of anti-inflammatory ingredients, perfect for starting your day with a refreshing and health-boosting drink.

### Equipment

Blender, Measuring Cups, Measuring Spoons

### Ingredients

- 1 cup unsweetened almond milk
- 1 cup frozen pineapple chunks
- 1 banana
- 1 tsp fresh ginger, grated
- 1 tsp ground turmeric
- 1 tbsp honey (optional)
- 1 tbsp chia seeds
- 1/2 tsp ground cinnamon
- 1/2 cup ice cubes

### Directions

1. Combine almond milk, pineapple, and banana in a blender.
2. Add ginger, turmeric, honey, chia seeds, and cinnamon.
3. Blend on high until smooth and creamy.
4. Add ice cubes and blend again until the ice is crushed and the smoothie is frothy.
5. Pour into glasses and serve immediately.

### Nutritional Information

Calories: 180, Protein: 3g, Carbohydrates: 40g, Fat: 3g, Fiber: 6g, Cholesterol: 0mg, Sodium: 80mg, Potassium: 450mg

# FLUFFY OAT & BANANA PANCAKES

**Servings 4 | Prep: 10 min | Cook: 15 min**

These fluffy oat and banana pancakes are a delightful way to start your day, offering a nutritious and satisfying breakfast option that is both wholesome and delicious.

### Equipment

Blender, Non-stick skillet, Spatula

### Ingredients

- 1 cup rolled oats
- 2 ripe bananas
- 2 large eggs
- 1/2 cup almond milk
- 1 tsp baking powder
- 1/2 tsp vanilla extract
- 1/4 tsp cinnamon
- Pinch of salt
- Cooking spray or a small amount of coconut oil for the skillet

### Directions

1. Blend the rolled oats in a blender until they form a fine flour.
2. Add the bananas, eggs, almond milk, baking powder, vanilla extract, cinnamon, and salt to the blender. Blend until smooth.
3. Heat a non-stick skillet over medium heat and lightly coat with cooking spray or coconut oil.
4. Pour 1/4 cup of the batter onto the skillet for each pancake. Cook until bubbles form on the surface, about 2-3 minutes.
5. Flip the pancakes and cook for another 2-3 minutes until golden brown.
6. Repeat with the remaining batter, adding more oil to the skillet as needed.
7. Serve warm with your favorite toppings such as fresh berries or a drizzle of maple syrup.

### Nutritional Information

Calories: 210, Protein: 6g, Carbohydrates: 36g, Fat: 5g, Fiber: 4g, Cholesterol: 55 mg, Sodium: 150 mg, Potassium: 420 mg

## SWEET POTATO & CINNAMON BREAKFAST HASH

**Servings 4 | Prep: 10 min | Cook: 20 min**

This breakfast hash combines the natural sweetness of sweet potatoes with the warm spice of cinnamon, creating a comforting and nutritious start to your day.

### Equipment

Skillet, Spatula, Knife

### Ingredients

- 2 tbsp olive oil
- 1 lb sweet potatoes, peeled and diced
- 1 medium onion, diced
- 1 red bell pepper, diced
- 1 tsp ground cinnamon
- 1/2 tsp salt
- 1/4 tsp black pepper
- 2 tbsp fresh parsley, chopped

### Directions

1. Heat olive oil in a skillet over medium heat.
2. Add diced sweet potatoes and cook for 10 minutes, stirring occasionally.
3. Add onion and red bell pepper to the skillet; cook for another 5 minutes.
4. Sprinkle cinnamon, salt, and black pepper over the mixture; stir well.
5. Continue cooking until sweet potatoes are tender, about 5 more minutes.
6. Garnish with fresh parsley before serving.

### Nutritional Information

Calories: 180, Protein: 2g, Carbohydrates: 28g, Fat: 7g, Fiber: 5g, Cholesterol: 0mg, Sodium: 310mg, Potassium: 450mg

## PROTEIN-PACKED GREEK YOGURT PARFAIT

**Servings 2 | Prep: 10 min | Cook: 0 min**

This parfait is a delightful blend of creamy Greek yogurt, fresh berries, and crunchy granola, perfect for a nutritious start to your day.

### Equipment

Mixing Bowl, Spoon, Parfait Glasses

### Ingredients

- 1 cup Greek yogurt
- 1/2 cup mixed berries (such as blueberries, strawberries, and raspberries)
- 1/4 cup granola
- 1 tbsp honey
- 1 tbsp chia seeds
- 1/2 tsp vanilla extract

### Directions

1. In a mixing bowl, combine Greek yogurt, honey, and vanilla extract. Stir until smooth.
2. Layer half of the yogurt mixture into the bottom of two parfait glasses.
3. Add a layer of mixed berries over the yogurt in each glass.
4. Sprinkle chia seeds evenly over the berries.
5. Add a layer of granola on top of the berries.
6. Repeat the layers with the remaining yogurt, berries, and granola.
7. Serve immediately or refrigerate for up to 2 hours for a chilled parfait.

### Nutritional Information

Calories: 250, Protein: 14g, Carbohydrates: 35g, Fat: 7g, Fiber: 5g, Cholesterol: 5mg, Sodium: 60mg, Potassium: 300mg

# APPLE CINNAMON BAKED OATMEAL

**Servings 6 | Prep: 10 min | Cook: 35 min**

This warm and comforting Apple Cinnamon Baked Oatmeal is perfect for a cozy breakfast. It's packed with wholesome ingredients and the delightful aroma of cinnamon and apples.

### Equipment

Baking Dish, Mixing Bowl, Whisk

### Ingredients

- 2 cups rolled oats
- 1 ½ cups almond milk
- 2 large apples, peeled and diced
- 2 tbsp maple syrup
- 1 tsp ground cinnamon
- 1 tsp vanilla extract
- ½ tsp baking powder
- ¼ tsp salt
- 2 tbsp chopped walnuts (optional)

### Directions

1. Preheat the oven to 350°F (175°C). Grease a baking dish lightly.
2. In a mixing bowl, combine oats, baking powder, cinnamon, and salt.
3. Add almond milk, maple syrup, and vanilla extract to the dry ingredients. Mix well.
4. Fold in the diced apples and pour the mixture into the prepared baking dish.
5. Sprinkle walnuts on top if using.
6. Bake for 35 minutes or until the top is golden and the oatmeal is set.
7. Let it cool slightly before serving. Enjoy warm.

### Nutritional Information

Calories: 210, Protein: 5g, Carbohydrates: 38g, Fat: 5g, Fiber: 5g, Cholesterol: 0mg, Sodium: 120mg, Potassium: 220mg

# SUPERFOOD ACAI SMOOTHIE BOWL

**Servings 2 | Prep: 10 min | Cook: 0 min**

This vibrant and nutrient-packed acai smoothie bowl is a perfect way to kickstart your day with a burst of energy and antioxidants.

### Equipment

Blender, Measuring Cups, Spoon

### Ingredients

- 3.5 oz frozen acai puree
- 1 banana, sliced
- 1/2 cup almond milk
- 1/4 cup blueberries
- 1 tbsp chia seeds
- 1 tbsp honey (optional)
- 1/4 cup granola
- 1/4 cup sliced strawberries
- 2 tbsp shredded coconut

### Directions

1. Blend the frozen acai puree, banana, almond milk, blueberries, chia seeds, and honey in a blender until smooth.
2. Pour the smoothie mixture into two bowls.
3. Top each bowl with granola, sliced strawberries, and shredded coconut.
4. Serve immediately and enjoy the refreshing taste.

### Nutritional Information

Calories: 250, Protein: 4g, Carbohydrates: 45g, Fat: 8g, Fiber: 9g, Cholesterol: 0mg, Sodium: 60mg, Potassium: 450mg

# BLUEBERRY & ALMOND BUTTER SMOOTHIE

**Servings 2 | Prep: 5 min | Cook: 0 min**

This creamy and refreshing smoothie combines the antioxidant power of blueberries with the rich, nutty flavor of almond butter, making it a perfect start to your day or a revitalizing snack.

### Equipment

Blender, Measuring Cups, Measuring Spoons

### Ingredients

- 1 cup fresh or frozen blueberries
- 2 tablespoons almond butter
- 1 cup unsweetened almond milk
- 1 tablespoon chia seeds
- 1 teaspoon honey (optional)
- 1/2 teaspoon vanilla extract
- 1/2 cup ice cubes

### Directions

1. Add the blueberries, almond butter, and almond milk to the blender.
2. Sprinkle in the chia seeds and add honey and vanilla extract for sweetness and flavor.
3. Top with ice cubes to achieve your desired consistency.
4. Blend on high speed until smooth and creamy.
5. Pour into glasses and serve immediately.

### Nutritional Information

Calories: 210, Protein: 5g, Carbohydrates: 24g, Fat: 12g, Fiber: 7g, Cholesterol: 0mg, Sodium: 80mg, Potassium: 290mg

# COCONUT & PINEAPPLE TROPICAL SMOOTHIE

**Servings 2 | Prep: 5 min | Cook: 0 min**

Dive into a refreshing blend of tropical flavors with this Coconut & Pineapple Tropical Smoothie. Perfect for a quick breakfast or a revitalizing snack, this smoothie brings the essence of the tropics to your glass.

### Equipment

Blender, Measuring Cups, Measuring Spoons

### Ingredients

- 1 cup fresh pineapple chunks
- 1 cup coconut milk
- 1/2 cup Greek yogurt
- 1 tablespoon honey
- 1/2 teaspoon vanilla extract
- 1/2 cup ice cubes

### Directions

1. Combine pineapple chunks, coconut milk, Greek yogurt, honey, and vanilla extract in a blender.
2. Add ice cubes to the blender.
3. Blend on high speed until smooth and creamy.
4. Pour into glasses and serve immediately.
5. Garnish with a pineapple slice or shredded coconut, if desired.

### Nutritional Information

Calories: 210, Protein: 5g, Carbohydrates: 30g, Fat: 10g, Fiber: 2g, Cholesterol: 5mg, Sodium: 40mg, Potassium: 250mg

# VANILLA CHIA PUDDING WITH MANGO

**Servings 4 | Prep: 10 min | Cook: 0 min**

This creamy vanilla chia pudding topped with fresh mango is a refreshing and nutritious way to start your day. Packed with fiber and healthy fats, it's a perfect blend of taste and health.

### Equipment

Mixing Bowl, Whisk, Measuring Cups, Refrigerator

### Ingredients

- 1 cup unsweetened almond milk
- 1/4 cup chia seeds
- 1 tbsp pure maple syrup
- 1 tsp vanilla extract
- 1 cup diced fresh mango
- 1/4 cup unsweetened shredded coconut (optional)

### Directions

1. In a mixing bowl, whisk together the almond milk, chia seeds, maple syrup, and vanilla extract until well combined.
2. Cover the bowl and refrigerate for at least 4 hours or overnight, allowing the chia seeds to absorb the liquid and thicken.
3. Once set, stir the pudding to ensure even consistency.
4. Divide the chia pudding into four serving bowls or jars.
5. Top each serving with diced mango and a sprinkle of shredded coconut, if desired.

### Nutritional Information

Calories: 150, Protein: 3g, Carbohydrates: 22g, Fat: 7g, Fiber: 6g, Cholesterol: 0mg, Sodium: 45mg, Potassium: 180mg

# HOMEMADE BUCKWHEAT GRANOLA WITH NUTS

**Servings 8 | Prep: 10 min | Cook: 30 min**

This crunchy and nutty buckwheat granola is a perfect start to your day, offering a wholesome and satisfying breakfast option that's both delicious and nutritious.

### Equipment

Baking Sheet, Mixing Bowl, Parchment Paper

### Ingredients

- 2 cups buckwheat groats
- 1 cup rolled oats
- 1/2 cup almonds, chopped
- 1/2 cup walnuts, chopped
- 1/4 cup sunflower seeds
- 1/4 cup pumpkin seeds
- 1/4 cup honey
- 2 tbsp coconut oil, melted
- 1 tsp vanilla extract
- 1/2 tsp cinnamon
- 1/4 tsp salt

### Directions

1. Preheat the oven to 325°F (165°C) and line a baking sheet with parchment paper.
2. In a large mixing bowl, combine buckwheat groats, rolled oats, almonds, walnuts, sunflower seeds, and pumpkin seeds.
3. In a small bowl, whisk together honey, melted coconut oil, vanilla extract, cinnamon, and salt.
4. Pour the wet mixture over the dry ingredients and stir until everything is well coated.
5. Spread the mixture evenly on the prepared baking sheet.
6. Bake for 25-30 minutes, stirring halfway through, until golden brown.
7. Allow to cool completely before storing in an airtight container.

### Nutritional Information

Calories: 250, Protein: 6g, Carbohydrates: 32g, Fat: 12g, Fiber: 4g, Cholesterol: 0mg, Sodium: 50mg, Potassium: 180mg

# CARROT CAKE OVERNIGHT OATS

**Servings 2 | Prep: 10 min | Cook: 0 min**

This delightful recipe combines the flavors of carrot cake with the convenience of overnight oats, offering a nutritious and delicious start to your day.

### Equipment

Mixing Bowl, Grater, Mason Jars or Containers

### Ingredients

- 1 cup rolled oats
- 1 cup unsweetened almond milk
- 1/2 cup grated carrots
- 1/4 cup Greek yogurt
- 2 tbsp maple syrup
- 1 tsp vanilla extract
- 1/2 tsp ground cinnamon
- 1/4 tsp ground nutmeg
- 2 tbsp chopped walnuts
- 2 tbsp raisins

### Directions

1. In a mixing bowl, combine rolled oats, almond milk, Greek yogurt, and maple syrup.
2. Add grated carrots, vanilla extract, ground cinnamon, and ground nutmeg to the mixture. Stir well.
3. Fold in chopped walnuts and raisins until evenly distributed.
4. Divide the mixture into mason jars or containers, cover, and refrigerate overnight.
5. In the morning, give the oats a good stir and enjoy cold or warmed up.

### Nutritional Information

Calories: 320, Protein: 9g, Carbohydrates: 50g, Fat: 10g, Fiber: 7g, Cholesterol: 5mg, Sodium: 60mg, Potassium: 450mg

# STRAWBERRY & COCONUT CHIA PUDDING

**Servings 4 | Prep: 10 min | Cook: 0 min**

This delightful Strawberry & Coconut Chia Pudding is a refreshing and nutritious way to start your day. Packed with the natural sweetness of strawberries and the creamy texture of coconut milk, it's a perfect blend of flavors and health benefits.

### Equipment

Mixing Bowl, Whisk, Refrigerator

### Ingredients

- 1 cup coconut milk
- 1/2 cup chia seeds
- 1 cup strawberries, hulled and sliced
- 2 tbsp honey or maple syrup
- 1 tsp vanilla extract
- 1/4 cup unsweetened shredded coconut

### Directions

1. In a mixing bowl, combine coconut milk, chia seeds, honey, and vanilla extract. Whisk until well combined.
2. Cover the bowl and refrigerate for at least 4 hours or overnight, allowing the chia seeds to absorb the liquid and thicken.
3. Once set, stir the pudding to ensure an even consistency.
4. Divide the pudding into serving bowls and top with sliced strawberries and shredded coconut.
5. Serve immediately or store in the refrigerator for up to 3 days.

### Nutritional Information

Calories: 220, Protein: 4g, Carbohydrates: 25g, Fat: 12g, Fiber: 8g, Cholesterol: 0mg, Sodium: 20mg, Potassium: 300mg

## PEANUT BUTTER & CACAO POWER SMOOTHIE

**Servings 2 | Prep: 5 min | Cook: 0 min**

This energizing smoothie combines the rich flavors of peanut butter and cacao, offering a deliciously creamy and nutritious start to your day.

### Equipment

Blender, Measuring Cups, Measuring Spoons

### Ingredients

- 1 cup unsweetened almond milk
- 2 tablespoons natural peanut butter
- 1 tablespoon raw cacao powder
- 1 banana, frozen
- 1 tablespoon chia seeds
- 1 teaspoon honey (optional)
- 1/2 teaspoon vanilla extract
- Ice cubes (optional, for a thicker consistency)

### Directions

1. Add almond milk, peanut butter, and cacao powder to the blender.
2. Break the frozen banana into chunks and add to the blender.
3. Sprinkle in chia seeds, honey, and vanilla extract.
4. Blend on high until smooth and creamy.
5. Add ice cubes if desired and blend again until well combined.
6. Pour into glasses and serve immediately.

### Nutritional Information

Calories: 250, Protein: 7g, Carbohydrates: 30g, Fat: 12g, Fiber: 7g, Cholesterol: 0mg, Sodium: 120mg, Potassium: 550mg

## SPICED QUINOA PORRIDGE WITH APPLES

**Servings 4 | Prep: 10 min | Cook: 20 min**

This warm and comforting spiced quinoa porridge is a perfect start to your day, combining the nutty flavor of quinoa with the sweetness of apples and a hint of cinnamon.

### Equipment

Medium Saucepan, Wooden Spoon, Measuring Cups and Spoons

### Ingredients

- 1 cup quinoa, rinsed
- 2 cups water
- 1 cup unsweetened almond milk
- 1 large apple, peeled, cored, and diced
- 2 tbsp maple syrup
- 1 tsp ground cinnamon
- 1/4 tsp ground nutmeg
- 1/4 tsp salt
- 1/4 cup chopped walnuts (optional)

### Directions

1. In a medium saucepan, combine quinoa and water. Bring to a boil over medium-high heat.
2. Reduce heat to low, cover, and simmer for 15 minutes or until quinoa is tender and water is absorbed.
3. Stir in almond milk, diced apple, maple syrup, cinnamon, nutmeg, and salt. Cook for an additional 5 minutes, stirring occasionally.
4. Remove from heat and let sit for a few minutes to thicken.
5. Serve warm, topped with chopped walnuts if desired.

### Nutritional Information

Calories: 220, Protein: 6g, Carbohydrates: 38g, Fat: 6g, Fiber: 5g, Cholesterol: 0mg, Sodium: 150mg, Potassium: 350mg

# GREEN APPLE & KALE SMOOTHIE

**Servings 2 | Prep: 10 min | Cook: 0 min**

This vibrant smoothie combines the crispness of green apples with the nutrient-rich goodness of kale, creating a refreshing and energizing start to your day.

### Equipment

Blender, Measuring Cups, Knife

### Ingredients

- 1 cup kale leaves, packed
- 1 medium green apple, cored and chopped
- 1 banana, peeled
- 1 cup unsweetened almond milk
- 1 tablespoon chia seeds
- 1 tablespoon honey (optional)
- 1/2 cup ice cubes

### Directions

1. Add the kale leaves, green apple, banana, and almond milk to the blender.
2. Sprinkle in the chia seeds and add honey if desired for sweetness.
3. Top with ice cubes to chill the smoothie.
4. Blend on high speed until smooth and creamy.
5. Pour into glasses and serve immediately.

### Nutritional Information

Calories: 150, Protein: 3g, Carbohydrates: 35g, Fat: 2g, Fiber: 6g, Cholesterol: 0mg, Sodium: 60mg, Potassium: 450mg

# GOLDEN MILK TURMERIC SMOOTHIE

**Servings 2 | Prep: 5 min | Cook: 0 min**

A vibrant and nourishing smoothie that combines the anti-inflammatory benefits of turmeric with the creamy richness of coconut milk, perfect for a refreshing and health-boosting start to your day.

### Equipment

Blender, Measuring Cups, Measuring Spoons

### Ingredients

- 1 cup unsweetened coconut milk
- 1 banana, frozen
- 1 tbsp turmeric powder
- 1 tsp ground cinnamon
- 1 tsp honey (optional)
- 1/2 tsp vanilla extract
- 1/4 tsp ground ginger
- 1/4 tsp black pepper
- 1/2 cup ice cubes

### Directions

1. Add the coconut milk and frozen banana to the blender.
2. Sprinkle in the turmeric powder, ground cinnamon, and ground ginger.
3. Add honey and vanilla extract for sweetness, if desired.
4. Include black pepper to enhance turmeric absorption.
5. Toss in the ice cubes for a chilled texture.
6. Blend on high until smooth and creamy.
7. Pour into glasses and serve immediately.

### Nutritional Information

Calories: 150, Protein: 2g, Carbohydrates: 30g, Fat: 4g, Fiber: 4g, Cholesterol: 0mg, Sodium: 20mg, Potassium: 450mg

# MATCHA ENERGY BOOSTING SMOOTHIE

**Servings 2 | Prep: 5 min | Cook: 0 min**

This vibrant smoothie is a perfect morning pick-me-up, combining the antioxidant power of matcha with the creamy goodness of almond milk and banana for a refreshing start to your day.

### Equipment

Blender, Measuring Cups, Measuring Spoons

### Ingredients

- 1 cup unsweetened almond milk
- 1 tsp matcha green tea powder
- 1 banana, frozen
- 1 tbsp chia seeds
- 1 tbsp honey (optional)
- 1/2 cup ice cubes

### Directions

1. Add almond milk and matcha powder to the blender.
2. Peel and slice the frozen banana, then add it to the blender.
3. Add chia seeds, honey, and ice cubes.
4. Blend on high speed until smooth and creamy.
5. Pour into glasses and serve immediately.

### Nutritional Information

Calories: 150, Protein: 3g, Carbohydrates: 30g, Fat: 3g, Fiber: 5g, Cholesterol: 0mg, Sodium: 60mg, Potassium: 450mg

# AVOCADO & BERRY BREAKFAST TOAST

**Servings 2 | Prep: 10 min | Cook: 0 min**

This vibrant and nutritious toast combines creamy avocado with the sweet and tangy flavors of fresh berries, making it a perfect start to your day.

### Equipment

Toaster, Knife, Cutting Board

### Ingredients

- 2 slices whole-grain bread
- 1 ripe avocado
- 1/2 cup mixed berries (such as strawberries, blueberries, and raspberries)
- 1 tbsp honey
- 1 tsp chia seeds
- Pinch of sea salt

### Directions

1. Toast the whole-grain bread slices to your desired level of crispiness.
2. While the bread is toasting, halve the avocado, remove the pit, and scoop the flesh into a bowl.
3. Mash the avocado with a fork until smooth, then add a pinch of sea salt.
4. Spread the mashed avocado evenly over each slice of toasted bread.
5. Top with mixed berries and drizzle with honey.
6. Sprinkle chia seeds over the top for added texture and nutrition.

### Nutritional Information

Calories: 250, Protein: 5g, Carbohydrates: 35g, Fat: 12g, Fiber: 9g, Cholesterol: 0mg, Sodium: 150mg, Potassium: 450mg

# CHOCOLATE ALMOND BUTTER PROTEIN SHAKE

**Servings 2 | Prep: 5 min | Cook: 0 min**

Indulge in a creamy, protein-packed shake that combines the rich flavors of chocolate and almond butter, perfect for a nutritious start to your day or a post-workout boost.

### Equipment

Blender, Measuring Cups, Measuring Spoons

### Ingredients

- 2 cups unsweetened almond milk
- 2 tbsp almond butter
- 2 tbsp unsweetened cocoa powder
- 1 banana, frozen
- 1 scoop chocolate protein powder
- 1 tsp vanilla extract
- 1 tbsp chia seeds (optional)
- Ice cubes (optional, for thicker consistency)

### Directions

1. Add the almond milk, almond butter, and cocoa powder to the blender.
2. Break the frozen banana into chunks and add to the blender.
3. Add the chocolate protein powder, vanilla extract, and chia seeds.
4. Blend on high until smooth and creamy.
5. Add ice cubes if desired and blend again until the desired consistency is reached.
6. Pour into glasses and serve immediately.

### Nutritional Information

Calories: 250, Protein: 15g, Carbohydrates: 30g, Fat: 10g, Fiber: 6g, Cholesterol: 0mg, Sodium: 150mg, Potassium: 600mg

# CREAMY OATMEAL WITH FLAXSEEDS & WALNUTS

**Servings 2 | Prep: 5 min | Cook: 10 min**

This creamy oatmeal is a nourishing start to your day, packed with the goodness of flaxseeds and walnuts for a satisfying crunch and a boost of omega-3s.

### Equipment

Medium saucepan, Wooden spoon, Measuring cups and spoons

### Ingredients

- 1 cup rolled oats
- 2 cups water
- 1/2 cup almond milk
- 2 tbsp flaxseeds
- 1/4 cup walnuts, chopped
- 1 tbsp honey (optional)
- 1/2 tsp cinnamon
- 1/4 tsp salt

### Directions

1. In a medium saucepan, combine the rolled oats, water, and salt. Bring to a boil over medium heat.
2. Reduce the heat to low and simmer, stirring occasionally, until the oats are creamy and tender, about 5 minutes.
3. Stir in the almond milk, flaxseeds, and cinnamon. Cook for an additional 2-3 minutes until heated through.
4. Remove from heat and stir in the chopped walnuts and honey, if using.
5. Divide the oatmeal into bowls and serve warm.

### Nutritional Information

Calories: 320, Protein: 9g, Carbohydrates: 45g, Fat: 14g, Fiber: 8g, Cholesterol: 0mg, Sodium: 150mg, Potassium: 250mg

# DATE & NUT SUPERFOOD BREAKFAST BARS

**Servings 8 | Prep: 15 min | Cook: 20 min**

These nutrient-packed breakfast bars are perfect for a quick morning boost or a healthy snack. Loaded with dates, nuts, and seeds, they offer a deliciously chewy texture and a natural sweetness that satisfies.

### Equipment

Baking Pan, Food Processor, Mixing Bowl

### Ingredients

- 1 cup pitted dates
- 1 cup raw almonds
- 1/2 cup walnuts
- 1/4 cup chia seeds
- 1/4 cup flaxseeds
- 1/4 cup unsweetened shredded coconut
- 1/4 cup honey
- 1 tsp vanilla extract
- 1/2 tsp cinnamon
- 1/4 tsp salt

### Directions

1. Preheat the oven to 350°F (175°C) and line a baking pan with parchment paper.
2. In a food processor, pulse the dates until they form a sticky paste.
3. In a mixing bowl, combine the date paste with almonds, walnuts, chia seeds, flaxseeds, shredded coconut, honey, vanilla extract, cinnamon, and salt. Mix well.
4. Press the mixture evenly into the prepared baking pan.
5. Bake for 20 minutes or until the edges are golden brown.
6. Allow to cool completely before cutting into bars.

### Nutritional Information

Calories: 220, Protein: 5g, Carbohydrates: 28g, Fat: 12g, Fiber: 5g, Cholesterol: 0mg, Sodium: 50mg, Potassium: 250mg

# LEMON BLUEBERRY PROTEIN PANCAKES

**Servings 4 | Prep: 10 min | Cook: 15 min**

These Lemon Blueberry Protein Pancakes are a delightful way to start your day, combining the tangy zest of lemon with the sweet burst of blueberries, all while packing a protein punch to keep you energized.

### Equipment

Non-stick skillet, Mixing bowl, Whisk

### Ingredients

- 1 cup oat flour
- 1 scoop (about 1 oz) vanilla protein powder
- 1 tsp baking powder
- 1/2 tsp baking soda
- 1/4 tsp salt
- 1 cup unsweetened almond milk
- 1 large egg
- 1 tbsp lemon juice
- 1 tsp lemon zest
- 1 tbsp honey
- 1/2 cup fresh blueberries
- Cooking spray or 1 tsp coconut oil

### Directions

1. In a mixing bowl, whisk together oat flour, protein powder, baking powder, baking soda, and salt.
2. In another bowl, combine almond milk, egg, lemon juice, lemon zest, and honey. Mix well.
3. Gradually add the wet ingredients to the dry ingredients, stirring until just combined. Fold in the blueberries.
4. Heat a non-stick skillet over medium heat and lightly coat with cooking spray or coconut oil.
5. Pour 1/4 cup of batter onto the skillet for each pancake. Cook until bubbles form on the surface, then flip and cook until golden brown.
6. Serve warm, optionally with a drizzle of honey or a sprinkle of additional blueberries.

### Nutritional Information

Calories: 210, Protein: 12g, Carbohydrates: 30g, Fat: 5g, Fiber: 4g, Cholesterol: 45mg, Sodium: 220mg, Potassium: 150mg

# Snacks & Energy Bites

# NO-BAKE ALMOND & DATE ENERGY BALLS

**Servings 12 | Prep: 15 min | Cook: 0 min**

These no-bake energy balls are a perfect blend of almonds and dates, providing a natural sweetness and a boost of energy. Ideal for a quick snack or post-workout fuel.

### Equipment

Food Processor, Mixing Bowl, Measuring Cups

### Ingredients

- 1 cup pitted Medjool dates
- 1 cup raw almonds
- 2 tbsp unsweetened cocoa powder
- 1 tbsp chia seeds
- 1 tsp vanilla extract
- 1/4 tsp sea salt
- 2 tbsp water (if needed)

### Directions

1. Combine dates and almonds in a food processor; pulse until finely chopped.
2. Add cocoa powder, chia seeds, vanilla extract, and sea salt; blend until the mixture is well combined and sticky.
3. If the mixture is too dry, add water one tablespoon at a time until it holds together.
4. Roll the mixture into 1-inch balls using your hands.
5. Place the energy balls in a container and refrigerate for at least 30 minutes before serving.

### Nutritional Information

Calories: 110, Protein: 3g, Carbohydrates: 15g, Fat: 5g, Fiber: 3g, Cholesterol: 0mg, Sodium: 25mg, Potassium: 180mg

# SPICED CHICKPEA CRUNCHIES

**Servings 4 | Prep: 10 min | Cook: 30 min**

These Spiced Chickpea Crunchies are a delightful, protein-packed snack with a satisfying crunch and a hint of spice, perfect for clean eating enthusiasts.

### Equipment

Baking Sheet, Mixing Bowl, Parchment Paper

### Ingredients

- 1 can (15 oz) chickpeas, drained and rinsed
- 1 tbsp olive oil
- 1 tsp ground cumin
- 1 tsp smoked paprika
- 1/2 tsp garlic powder
- 1/4 tsp cayenne pepper (optional, for extra heat)
- 1/2 tsp sea salt

### Directions

1. Preheat the oven to 400°F (200°C) and line a baking sheet with parchment paper.
2. In a mixing bowl, combine chickpeas, olive oil, cumin, smoked paprika, garlic powder, cayenne pepper, and sea salt. Toss until chickpeas are evenly coated.
3. Spread the chickpeas in a single layer on the prepared baking sheet.
4. Bake for 25-30 minutes, stirring halfway through, until chickpeas are golden and crispy.
5. Allow to cool slightly before serving.

### Nutritional Information

Calories: 120, Protein: 5g, Carbohydrates: 18g, Fat: 4g, Fiber: 5g, Cholesterol: 0mg, Sodium: 300mg, Potassium: 200mg

# SUPERFOOD TRAIL MIX WITH CACAO NIBS

### Servings 8 | Prep: 10 min | Cook: 0 min

A nutrient-packed snack that combines the richness of cacao nibs with the wholesome goodness of nuts and dried fruits, perfect for on-the-go energy.

### Equipment

Mixing Bowl, Measuring Cups, Airtight Container

### Ingredients

- 1 cup raw almonds
- 1 cup raw cashews
- 1/2 cup cacao nibs
- 1/2 cup dried goji berries
- 1/2 cup unsweetened coconut flakes
- 1/4 cup pumpkin seeds
- 1/4 cup sunflower seeds

### Directions

1. In a large mixing bowl, combine the almonds, cashews, cacao nibs, goji berries, coconut flakes, pumpkin seeds, and sunflower seeds.
2. Stir the mixture until all ingredients are evenly distributed.
3. Transfer the trail mix to an airtight container for storage.
4. Store in a cool, dry place and enjoy as a snack whenever needed.

### Nutritional Information

Calories: 210, Protein: 5g, Carbohydrates: 15g, Fat: 15g, Fiber: 4g, Cholesterol: 0mg, Sodium: 5mg, Potassium: 250mg

# HOMEMADE FLAXSEED CRACKERS

### Servings 4 | Prep: 10 min | Cook: 25 min

These homemade flaxseed crackers are a crunchy, nutritious snack perfect for clean eating. Packed with fiber and omega-3s, they are both satisfying and healthy.

### Equipment

Mixing Bowl, Baking Sheet, Parchment Paper

### Ingredients

- 1 cup flaxseeds
- 1/2 cup water
- 1/2 tsp sea salt
- 1/2 tsp garlic powder
- 1/2 tsp onion powder

### Directions

1. Preheat the oven to 350°F (175°C) and line a baking sheet with parchment paper.
2. In a mixing bowl, combine flaxseeds, water, sea salt, garlic powder, and onion powder. Stir until well mixed.
3. Let the mixture sit for 5 minutes to thicken.
4. Spread the mixture evenly onto the prepared baking sheet, pressing it down to about 1/8-inch thickness.
5. Bake for 25 minutes or until the edges are golden brown and the center is firm.
6. Allow to cool completely, then break into pieces.

### Nutritional Information

Calories: 150, Protein: 5g, Carbohydrates: 8g, Fat: 11g, Fiber: 7g, Cholesterol: 0mg, Sodium: 150mg, Potassium: 200mg

# ROASTED CINNAMON ALMONDS

**Servings 8 | Prep: 10 min | Cook: 20 min**

These roasted cinnamon almonds are a delightful blend of sweet and spicy, perfect for a quick snack or energy boost. The aroma of cinnamon and the crunch of almonds make them irresistible.

### Equipment

Baking Sheet, Mixing Bowl, Parchment Paper

### Ingredients

- 2 cups raw almonds
- 1/4 cup pure maple syrup
- 1 tbsp ground cinnamon
- 1/2 tsp sea salt
- 1 tsp vanilla extract

### Directions

1. Preheat your oven to 350°F (175°C) and line a baking sheet with parchment paper.
2. In a mixing bowl, combine the almonds, maple syrup, cinnamon, sea salt, and vanilla extract. Stir until the almonds are well coated.
3. Spread the almond mixture evenly on the prepared baking sheet.
4. Roast in the preheated oven for 15-20 minutes, stirring halfway through, until the almonds are golden and fragrant.
5. Remove from the oven and let them cool completely on the baking sheet before transferring to an airtight container.

### Nutritional Information

Calories: 210, Protein: 6g, Carbohydrates: 15g, Fat: 16g, Fiber: 4g, Cholesterol: 0mg, Sodium: 75mg, Potassium: 210mg

# CHIA SEED PROTEIN BARS

**Servings 12 | Prep: 15 min | Cook: 0 min**

These Chia Seed Protein Bars are a perfect blend of energy-boosting ingredients, offering a nutritious snack that's both satisfying and delicious. Packed with protein and fiber, they are ideal for a quick energy boost during the day.

### Equipment

Mixing Bowl, Measuring Cups, 8x8-inch Baking Dish, Parchment Paper

### Ingredients

- 1 cup rolled oats
- 1/2 cup chia seeds
- 1/2 cup almond butter
- 1/3 cup honey
- 1/4 cup protein powder (vanilla or unflavored)
- 1/4 cup unsweetened shredded coconut
- 1/4 cup dark chocolate chips
- 1 tsp vanilla extract
- 1/4 tsp sea salt

### Directions

1. Line an 8x8-inch baking dish with parchment paper, leaving some overhang for easy removal.
2. In a large mixing bowl, combine rolled oats, chia seeds, protein powder, shredded coconut, and sea salt.
3. In a separate bowl, mix almond butter, honey, and vanilla extract until smooth.
4. Pour the wet ingredients into the dry ingredients and stir until well combined.
5. Fold in the dark chocolate chips.
6. Press the mixture firmly into the prepared baking dish, ensuring an even layer.
7. Refrigerate for at least 1 hour or until set. Once firm, cut into 12 bars.

### Nutritional Information

Calories: 180, Protein: 6g, Carbohydrates: 20g, Fat: 9g, Fiber: 4g, Cholesterol: 0mg, Sodium: 50mg, Potassium: 120mg

# APPLE SLICES WITH ALMOND BUTTER & CINNAMON

**Servings 4 | Prep: 10 min | Cook: 0 min**

A simple yet delightful snack that combines the crispness of fresh apples with the creamy richness of almond butter, finished with a hint of cinnamon for a warm, comforting touch.

### Equipment

Knife, Cutting Board, Small Bowl

### Ingredients

- 2 medium apples, any variety
- 1/2 cup almond butter
- 1 tsp ground cinnamon
- 1 tbsp honey (optional)
- 1/4 cup chopped almonds (optional)

### Directions

1. Wash and core the apples, then slice them into thin wedges.
2. In a small bowl, mix the almond butter with honey if using, for added sweetness.
3. Spread a thin layer of almond butter on each apple slice.
4. Sprinkle ground cinnamon evenly over the almond butter-topped apple slices.
5. For added crunch, sprinkle chopped almonds over the top.
6. Serve immediately or store in an airtight container for up to 2 hours.

### Nutritional Information

Calories: 210, Protein: 5g, Carbohydrates: 27g, Fat: 12g, Fiber: 5g, Cholesterol: 0mg, Sodium: 2mg, Potassium: 250mg

# CARROT & HUMMUS WRAPS

**Servings 4 | Prep: 10 min | Cook: 0 min**

These Carrot & Hummus Wraps are a refreshing and nutritious snack, perfect for a quick bite or a light lunch. Packed with crunchy carrots and creamy hummus, they offer a delightful balance of flavors and textures.

### Equipment

Cutting Board, Knife, Spreader

### Ingredients

- 4 whole wheat tortillas (8-inch)
- 1 cup hummus
- 2 cups shredded carrots
- 1 cup baby spinach
- 1/2 cup sliced cucumbers
- 1/4 cup chopped fresh parsley
- 1 tablespoon lemon juice

### Directions

1. Lay each tortilla flat on the cutting board.
2. Spread 1/4 cup of hummus evenly over each tortilla.
3. Layer 1/2 cup of shredded carrots, 1/4 cup of baby spinach, and a few cucumber slices on top of the hummus.
4. Sprinkle chopped parsley and drizzle with a bit of lemon juice for added freshness.
5. Roll each tortilla tightly, tucking in the sides as you go.
6. Slice each wrap in half and serve immediately or wrap in foil for later.

### Nutritional Information

Calories: 210, Protein: 6g, Carbohydrates: 34g, Fat: 7g, Fiber: 7g, Cholesterol: 0mg, Sodium: 320mg, Potassium: 450mg

## OVEN-BAKED KALE CHIPS

**Servings 4 | Prep: 10 min | Cook: 15 min**

Crispy and light, these oven-baked kale chips are a perfect guilt-free snack that satisfies your craving for something crunchy and savory.

### Equipment

Baking Sheet, Parchment Paper, Mixing Bowl

### Ingredients

- 1 bunch kale (about 8 oz)
- 1 tbsp olive oil
- 1/2 tsp sea salt
- 1/4 tsp garlic powder (optional)

### Directions

1. Preheat the oven to 300°F (150°C). Line a baking sheet with parchment paper.
2. Wash and thoroughly dry the kale. Remove the stems and tear the leaves into bite-sized pieces.
3. In a mixing bowl, toss the kale with olive oil, sea salt, and garlic powder until evenly coated.
4. Spread the kale pieces in a single layer on the prepared baking sheet.
5. Bake for 15 minutes, or until the edges are crisp but not burnt.
6. Allow to cool slightly before serving.

### Nutritional Information

Calories: 60, Protein: 2g, Carbohydrates: 7g, Fat: 3.5g, Fiber: 2g, Cholesterol: 0mg, Sodium: 150mg, Potassium: 300mg

## QUINOA & PEANUT BUTTER ENERGY BITES

**Servings 12 | Prep: 15 min | Cook: 0 min**

These energy bites are a perfect blend of nutty quinoa and creamy peanut butter, offering a quick and nutritious snack to fuel your day.

### Equipment

Mixing Bowl, Measuring Cups, Spoon

### Ingredients

- 1 cup cooked quinoa
- 1/2 cup natural peanut butter
- 1/4 cup honey
- 1/2 cup rolled oats
- 1/4 cup mini chocolate chips
- 1/4 cup chia seeds
- 1 tsp vanilla extract

### Directions

1. In a mixing bowl, combine cooked quinoa, peanut butter, and honey until well blended.
2. Stir in rolled oats, mini chocolate chips, chia seeds, and vanilla extract.
3. Mix thoroughly until all ingredients are evenly distributed.
4. Using a spoon, scoop out small portions and roll them into 1-inch balls.
5. Place the energy bites on a tray and refrigerate for at least 30 minutes to set.

### Nutritional Information

Calories: 110, Protein: 3g, Carbohydrates: 14g, Fat: 5g, Fiber: 2g, Cholesterol: 0mg, Sodium: 30mg, Potassium: 100mg

# CRUNCHY ROASTED PUMPKIN SEEDS

**Servings 4 | Prep: 10 min | Cook: 25 min**

Enjoy a healthy and satisfying snack with these crunchy roasted pumpkin seeds, perfect for a quick energy boost or a nutritious treat.

### Equipment

Baking Sheet, Mixing Bowl, Oven

### Ingredients

- 1 cup raw pumpkin seeds
- 1 tbsp olive oil
- 1 tsp sea salt
- 1/2 tsp smoked paprika
- 1/4 tsp garlic powder

### Directions

1. Preheat the oven to 350°F (175°C).
2. In a mixing bowl, combine pumpkin seeds, olive oil, sea salt, smoked paprika, and garlic powder. Toss until seeds are evenly coated.
3. Spread the seasoned pumpkin seeds in a single layer on a baking sheet.
4. Roast in the preheated oven for 20-25 minutes, stirring halfway through, until golden brown and crunchy.
5. Allow to cool before serving or storing in an airtight container.

### Nutritional Information

Calories: 180, Protein: 8g, Carbohydrates: 4g, Fat: 15g, Fiber: 2g, Cholesterol: 0mg, Sodium: 290mg, Potassium: 230mg

# DARK CHOCOLATE & WALNUT BITES

**Servings 12 | Prep: 15 min | Cook: 0 min**

Indulge in these rich, nutty bites that combine the deep flavor of dark chocolate with the crunch of walnuts. Perfect for a quick energy boost or a guilt-free treat.

### Equipment

Food Processor, Mixing Bowl, Baking Sheet

### Ingredients

- 1 cup pitted dates
- 1 cup raw walnuts
- 1/2 cup dark chocolate chips (70% cacao or higher)
- 2 tbsp unsweetened cocoa powder
- 1 tbsp coconut oil
- 1 tsp vanilla extract
- 1/4 tsp sea salt

### Directions

1. In a food processor, combine the dates and walnuts. Pulse until finely chopped and well combined.
2. Add the dark chocolate chips, cocoa powder, coconut oil, vanilla extract, and sea salt to the mixture. Pulse until the mixture forms a sticky dough.
3. Using your hands, roll the mixture into 1-inch balls and place them on a baking sheet lined with parchment paper.
4. Refrigerate the bites for at least 30 minutes to allow them to firm up.
5. Store in an airtight container in the refrigerator for up to one week.

### Nutritional Information

Calories: 120, Protein: 2g, Carbohydrates: 15g, Fat: 8g, Fiber: 3g, Cholesterol: 0mg, Sodium: 30mg, Potassium: 150mg

# AVOCADO & TOMATO RICE CAKES

**Servings 4 | Prep: 10 min | Cook: 0 min**

These Avocado & Tomato Rice Cakes are a refreshing and satisfying snack, perfect for a quick energy boost. The creamy avocado pairs beautifully with the juicy tomatoes, all atop a crunchy rice cake.

### Equipment

Knife, Cutting Board, Spoon

### Ingredients

- 4 rice cakes
- 1 large avocado
- 1 cup cherry tomatoes, halved
- 1 tbsp lemon juice
- 1/4 tsp sea salt
- 1/4 tsp black pepper
- 1 tbsp fresh basil, chopped

### Directions

1. Halve the avocado, remove the pit, and scoop the flesh into a bowl.
2. Mash the avocado with a fork, then mix in the lemon juice, sea salt, and black pepper.
3. Spread the avocado mixture evenly over each rice cake.
4. Top each rice cake with halved cherry tomatoes.
5. Garnish with chopped fresh basil before serving.

### Nutritional Information

Calories: 150, Protein: 3g, Carbohydrates: 20g, Fat: 7g, Fiber: 5g, Cholesterol: 0mg, Sodium: 150mg, Potassium: 400mg

# COCONUT & CASHEW BLISS BALLS

**Servings 12 | Prep: 15 min | Cook: 0 min**

These delightful Coconut & Cashew Bliss Balls are the perfect clean-eating snack, combining the natural sweetness of dates with the creamy texture of cashews and a hint of coconut.

### Equipment

Food Processor, Mixing Bowl, Measuring Cups

### Ingredients

- 1 cup unsweetened shredded coconut
- 1 cup raw cashews
- 1 cup pitted Medjool dates
- 1 tbsp coconut oil
- 1 tsp vanilla extract
- 1/4 tsp sea salt

### Directions

1. In a food processor, combine the shredded coconut and cashews. Pulse until finely ground.
2. Add the pitted dates, coconut oil, vanilla extract, and sea salt to the processor. Blend until the mixture forms a sticky dough.
3. Scoop out tablespoon-sized portions of the mixture and roll them into balls using your hands.
4. Place the bliss balls on a plate or tray and refrigerate for at least 30 minutes to firm up.
5. Store in an airtight container in the refrigerator for up to a week.

### Nutritional Information

Calories: 120, Protein: 2g, Carbohydrates: 14g, Fat: 7g, Fiber: 2g, Cholesterol: 0mg, Sodium: 20mg, Potassium: 180mg

## NO-SUGAR APPLE CHIPS

**Servings 4 | Prep: 10 min | Cook: 120 min**

Crispy and naturally sweet, these no-sugar apple chips are a perfect guilt-free snack that captures the essence of clean eating.

### Equipment

Mandoline slicer, Baking sheet, Parchment paper

### Ingredients

- 2 large apples
- 1 tsp ground cinnamon

### Directions

1. Preheat your oven to 200°F (93°C) and line a baking sheet with parchment paper.
2. Using a mandoline slicer, thinly slice the apples into even rounds, about 1/8 inch thick.
3. Arrange the apple slices in a single layer on the prepared baking sheet.
4. Sprinkle the ground cinnamon evenly over the apple slices.
5. Bake in the preheated oven for 1 hour, then flip the slices and continue baking for another hour, or until crisp.
6. Remove from the oven and let them cool completely on a wire rack.

### Nutritional Information

Calories: 95, Protein: 0g, Carbohydrates: 25g, Fat: 0g, Fiber: 4g, Cholesterol: 0mg, Sodium: 1mg, Potassium: 195mg

## CUCUMBER & HUMMUS ROLL-UPS

**Servings 4 | Prep: 15 min | Cook: 0 min**

These refreshing cucumber and hummus roll-ups are a perfect blend of crisp and creamy, offering a delightful snack that's both nutritious and satisfying.

### Equipment

Mandoline slicer, Spreading knife, Toothpicks

### Ingredients

- 1 large cucumber
- 1 cup hummus
- 1/4 cup roasted red peppers, thinly sliced
- 1/4 cup fresh spinach leaves
- 1 tbsp lemon juice

### Directions

1. Wash the cucumber thoroughly and slice it lengthwise into thin strips using a mandoline slicer.
2. Spread a thin layer of hummus over each cucumber slice using a spreading knife.
3. Place a few slices of roasted red peppers and a couple of spinach leaves on top of the hummus.
4. Drizzle a small amount of lemon juice over the toppings for added zest.
5. Carefully roll up each cucumber slice and secure with a toothpick.
6. Serve immediately or refrigerate for up to 2 hours before serving.

### Nutritional Information

Calories: 90, Protein: 3g, Carbohydrates: 11g, Fat: 4g, Fiber: 3g, Cholesterol: 0mg, Sodium: 180mg, Potassium: 250mg

# PROTEIN-PACKED CHIA CRACKERS

**Servings 4 | Prep: 15 min | Cook: 25 min**

These crunchy chia crackers are a perfect protein-packed snack, combining wholesome seeds and spices for a nutritious bite.

### Equipment

Mixing Bowl, Baking Sheet, Parchment Paper

### Ingredients

- 1 cup almond flour
- 2 tbsp chia seeds
- 1 tbsp flaxseeds
- 1/4 cup water
- 1 tsp garlic powder
- 1/2 tsp sea salt
- 1 tbsp olive oil

### Directions

1. Preheat the oven to 350°F (175°C) and line a baking sheet with parchment paper.
2. In a mixing bowl, combine almond flour, chia seeds, flaxseeds, garlic powder, and sea salt.
3. Add water and olive oil to the dry ingredients, stirring until a dough forms.
4. Roll out the dough between two sheets of parchment paper to about 1/8-inch thickness.
5. Cut into desired cracker shapes and transfer to the prepared baking sheet.
6. Bake for 20-25 minutes, or until golden and crisp.
7. Allow to cool before serving.

### Nutritional Information

Calories: 150, Protein: 5g, Carbohydrates: 8g, Fat: 12g, Fiber: 4g, Cholesterol: 0mg, Sodium: 150mg, Potassium: 100mg

# SPICY EDAMAME SNACK BITES

**Servings 4 | Prep: 10 min | Cook: 5 min**

These Spicy Edamame Snack Bites are a perfect blend of heat and flavor, offering a nutritious and energizing snack option.

### Equipment

Medium saucepan, Mixing bowl, Baking sheet

### Ingredients

- 2 cups shelled edamame
- 1 tbsp olive oil
- 1 tsp chili powder
- 1/2 tsp garlic powder
- 1/4 tsp cayenne pepper
- 1/2 tsp sea salt
- 1 tbsp sesame seeds

### Directions

1. Preheat your oven to 375°F (190°C).
2. In a medium saucepan, bring water to a boil and add the edamame. Cook for 3 minutes, then drain.
3. In a mixing bowl, combine the cooked edamame, olive oil, chili powder, garlic powder, cayenne pepper, and sea salt. Toss until well coated.
4. Spread the edamame mixture evenly on a baking sheet.
5. Bake for 5 minutes, then sprinkle with sesame seeds and serve warm.

### Nutritional Information

Calories: 150, Protein: 9g, Carbohydrates: 12g, Fat: 8g, Fiber: 5g, Cholesterol: 0mg, Sodium: 300mg, Potassium: 450mg

# BANANA & ALMOND BUTTER RICE CAKES

**Servings 4 | Prep: 10 min | Cook: 0 min**

A delightful and nutritious snack that combines the creamy richness of almond butter with the natural sweetness of bananas, all atop a crunchy rice cake. Perfect for a quick energy boost or a light snack.

### Equipment

Butter knife, Cutting board, Measuring spoons

### Ingredients

- 4 rice cakes
- 4 tbsp almond butter
- 2 medium bananas
- 1 tbsp honey (optional)
- 1 tsp chia seeds (optional)

### Directions

1. Spread 1 tablespoon of almond butter evenly over each rice cake.
2. Slice the bananas into thin rounds on a cutting board.
3. Arrange banana slices on top of the almond butter-covered rice cakes.
4. Drizzle with honey for added sweetness, if desired.
5. Sprinkle chia seeds over the top for extra nutrition and crunch.

### Nutritional Information

Calories: 180, Protein: 4g, Carbohydrates: 28g, Fat: 8g, Fiber: 4g, Cholesterol: 0mg, Sodium: 30mg, Potassium: 300mg

# ROASTED SWEET POTATO WEDGES WITH PAPRIKA

**Servings 4 | Prep: 10 min | Cook: 30 min**

These roasted sweet potato wedges are a perfect blend of sweet and savory, with a hint of smoky paprika. They make a delicious and nutritious snack or side dish.

### Equipment

Baking Sheet, Mixing Bowl, Oven

### Ingredients

- 2 lbs sweet potatoes
- 2 tbsp olive oil
- 1 tsp smoked paprika
- 1/2 tsp garlic powder
- 1/2 tsp salt
- 1/4 tsp black pepper

### Directions

1. Preheat the oven to 425°F (220°C).
2. Wash and cut the sweet potatoes into wedges, leaving the skin on for extra fiber.
3. In a mixing bowl, combine olive oil, smoked paprika, garlic powder, salt, and black pepper.
4. Toss the sweet potato wedges in the spice mixture until evenly coated.
5. Arrange the wedges in a single layer on a baking sheet.
6. Roast in the oven for 25-30 minutes, turning halfway through, until golden brown and tender.
7. Serve warm and enjoy!

### Nutritional Information

Calories: 180, Protein: 2g, Carbohydrates: 32g, Fat: 7g, Fiber: 5g, Cholesterol: 0mg, Sodium: 300mg, Potassium: 450mg

## CRANBERRY & OAT GRANOLA BITES

**Servings 12 | Prep: 15 min | Cook: 0 min**

These no-bake Cranberry & Oat Granola Bites are the perfect blend of chewy and crunchy, offering a burst of natural sweetness from cranberries and a satisfying texture from oats. Ideal for a quick snack or energy boost on the go.

### Equipment

Mixing Bowl, Measuring Cups, Baking Sheet (for setting)

### Ingredients

- 1 1/2 cups rolled oats
- 1/2 cup dried cranberries
- 1/2 cup almond butter
- 1/4 cup honey
- 1/4 cup chopped almonds
- 1 tsp vanilla extract
- 1/2 tsp cinnamon

### Directions

1. In a mixing bowl, combine rolled oats, dried cranberries, and chopped almonds.
2. In a small saucepan over low heat, warm almond butter and honey until smooth. Stir in vanilla extract and cinnamon.
3. Pour the almond butter mixture over the oat mixture and stir until well combined.
4. Scoop tablespoon-sized portions and roll them into balls. Place on a baking sheet.
5. Refrigerate for at least 30 minutes to set before serving.

### Nutritional Information

Calories: 120, Protein: 3g, Carbohydrates: 16g, Fat: 6g, Fiber: 2g, Cholesterol: 0mg, Sodium: 2mg, Potassium: 100mg

## CARROT & ZUCCHINI MUFFINS

**Servings 12 | Prep: 15 min | Cook: 20 min**

These muffins are a delightful blend of sweet carrots and fresh zucchini, perfect for a nutritious snack or breakfast on the go.

### Equipment

Muffin Tin, Mixing Bowls, Grater

### Ingredients

- 1 cup grated carrots
- 1 cup grated zucchini
- 1 1/2 cups whole wheat flour
- 1/2 cup rolled oats
- 1/2 cup unsweetened applesauce
- 1/4 cup honey
- 2 large eggs
- 1 tsp vanilla extract
- 1 tsp baking powder
- 1/2 tsp baking soda
- 1/2 tsp cinnamon
- 1/4 tsp salt

### Directions

1. Preheat the oven to 350°F and line a muffin tin with paper liners.
2. In a large bowl, combine the grated carrots, zucchini, applesauce, honey, eggs, and vanilla extract. Mix well.
3. In another bowl, whisk together the flour, oats, baking powder, baking soda, cinnamon, and salt.
4. Gradually add the dry ingredients to the wet ingredients, stirring until just combined.
5. Spoon the batter evenly into the prepared muffin tin.
6. Bake for 18-20 minutes, or until a toothpick inserted into the center comes out clean.
7. Allow muffins to cool in the tin for 5 minutes before transferring to a wire rack to cool completely.

### Nutritional Information

Calories: 120, Protein: 3g, Carbohydrates: 22g, Fat: 2g, Fiber: 3g, Cholesterol: 30mg, Sodium: 150mg, Potassium: 150mg

# TURMERIC-SPICED MIXED NUTS

**Servings 8 | Prep: 5 min | Cook: 15 min**

A delightful blend of crunchy nuts coated in a vibrant turmeric spice mix, perfect for a healthy snack or energy boost.

### Equipment

Baking Sheet, Mixing Bowl, Spatula

### Ingredients

- 2 cups mixed nuts (almonds, cashews, walnuts)
- 1 tbsp olive oil
- 1 tsp ground turmeric
- 1/2 tsp ground cumin
- 1/2 tsp smoked paprika
- 1/4 tsp cayenne pepper (optional)
- 1/2 tsp sea salt
- 1 tbsp honey

### Directions

1. Preheat the oven to 350°F (175°C).
2. In a mixing bowl, combine olive oil, turmeric, cumin, smoked paprika, cayenne pepper, sea salt, and honey. Mix well.
3. Add the mixed nuts to the bowl and toss until they are evenly coated with the spice mixture.
4. Spread the nuts in a single layer on a baking sheet.
5. Bake for 12-15 minutes, stirring halfway through, until the nuts are golden and fragrant.
6. Allow to cool before serving or storing in an airtight container.

### Nutritional Information

Calories: 210, Protein: 5g, Carbohydrates: 10g, Fat: 18g, Fiber: 3g, Cholesterol: 0mg, Sodium: 120mg, Potassium: 180mg

# STRAWBERRY & COCONUT YOGURT BARK

**Servings 8 | Prep: 10 min | Cook: 0 min**

This refreshing and creamy yogurt bark combines the natural sweetness of strawberries with the tropical flavor of coconut, making it a perfect clean-eating snack.

### Equipment

Baking Sheet, Parchment Paper, Mixing Bowl

### Ingredients

- 2 cups Greek yogurt
- 2 tbsp honey
- 1 tsp vanilla extract
- 1 cup strawberries, sliced
- 1/4 cup unsweetened shredded coconut

### Directions

1. Line a baking sheet with parchment paper.
2. In a mixing bowl, combine Greek yogurt, honey, and vanilla extract until smooth.
3. Spread the yogurt mixture evenly onto the prepared baking sheet.
4. Arrange sliced strawberries over the yogurt mixture.
5. Sprinkle shredded coconut on top.
6. Freeze for at least 3 hours or until completely set.
7. Break into pieces and serve immediately or store in the freezer for later.

### Nutritional Information

Calories: 90, Protein: 5g, Carbohydrates: 12g, Fat: 3g, Fiber: 1g, Cholesterol: 5mg, Sodium: 30mg, Potassium: 150mg

# HEMP SEED & HONEY PROTEIN BARS

**Servings 12 | Prep: 15 min | Cook: 0 min**

These protein bars are a perfect blend of nutty hemp seeds and sweet honey, offering a nutritious and energizing snack.

### Equipment

Mixing Bowl, Baking Pan, Parchment Paper

### Ingredients

- 1 cup rolled oats
- 1/2 cup hemp seeds
- 1/2 cup almond butter
- 1/3 cup honey
- 1/4 cup unsweetened shredded coconut
- 1/4 cup chopped almonds
- 1/4 cup dark chocolate chips
- 1 tsp vanilla extract
- 1/4 tsp sea salt

### Directions

1. Line a baking pan with parchment paper.
2. In a mixing bowl, combine oats, hemp seeds, shredded coconut, chopped almonds, and sea salt.
3. In a separate bowl, mix almond butter, honey, and vanilla extract until smooth.
4. Pour the wet mixture into the dry ingredients and stir until well combined.
5. Fold in the dark chocolate chips.
6. Press the mixture firmly into the prepared baking pan.
7. Refrigerate for at least 1 hour before slicing into bars.

### Nutritional Information

Calories: 210, Protein: 6g, Carbohydrates: 20g, Fat: 13g, Fiber: 3g, Cholesterol: 0mg, Sodium: 40mg, Potassium: 150mg

# CHEWY FIG & NUT SNACK BARS

**Servings 12 | Prep: 15 min | Cook: 0 min**

These chewy fig and nut snack bars are a perfect blend of natural sweetness and crunchy texture, providing a wholesome energy boost for any time of the day.

### Equipment

Food Processor, Mixing Bowl, 8x8-inch Baking Pan

### Ingredients

- 1 cup dried figs, stems removed
- 1 cup raw almonds
- 1/2 cup raw walnuts
- 1/4 cup unsweetened shredded coconut
- 2 tbsp chia seeds
- 2 tbsp honey
- 1 tsp vanilla extract
- 1/4 tsp sea salt

### Directions

1. Place the dried figs in a food processor and pulse until they form a sticky paste.
2. Add almonds, walnuts, shredded coconut, chia seeds, honey, vanilla extract, and sea salt to the food processor.
3. Pulse until the mixture is well combined and starts to clump together.
4. Line an 8x8-inch baking pan with parchment paper and press the mixture evenly into the pan.
5. Refrigerate for at least 1 hour to set.
6. Once set, remove from the pan and cut into 12 bars.
7. Store in an airtight container in the refrigerator for up to one week.

### Nutritional Information

Calories: 180, Protein: 4g, Carbohydrates: 22g, Fat: 10g, Fiber: 4g, Cholesterol: 0mg, Sodium: 30mg, Potassium: 220mg

# Salads & Dressings

# QUINOA & AVOCADO DETOX SALAD

**Servings 4 | Prep: 15 min | Cook: 15 min**

This refreshing quinoa and avocado detox salad is packed with nutrients and vibrant flavors, perfect for a clean eating lifestyle.

### Equipment

Medium Saucepan, Large Mixing Bowl, Whisk

### Ingredients

- 1 cup quinoa
- 2 cups water
- 1 avocado, diced
- 1 cup cherry tomatoes, halved
- 1 cucumber, diced
- 1/4 cup red onion, finely chopped
- 1/4 cup fresh cilantro, chopped
- 2 tbsp olive oil
- 1 tbsp lemon juice
- 1 tsp honey
- Salt and pepper to taste

### Directions

1. Rinse quinoa under cold water. In a medium saucepan, combine quinoa and water. Bring to a boil, reduce heat, cover, and simmer for 15 minutes or until water is absorbed. Fluff with a fork and let cool.
2. In a large mixing bowl, combine cooked quinoa, avocado, cherry tomatoes, cucumber, red onion, and cilantro.
3. In a small bowl, whisk together olive oil, lemon juice, honey, salt, and pepper.
4. Pour the dressing over the quinoa mixture and toss gently to combine.
5. Serve immediately or refrigerate for up to 2 hours to allow flavors to meld.

### Nutritional Information

Calories: 280, Protein: 6g, Carbohydrates: 35g, Fat: 14g, Fiber: 7g, Cholesterol: 0mg, Sodium: 10mg, Potassium: 600mg

# KALE & ROASTED CHICKPEA SALAD

**Servings 4 | Prep: 15 min | Cook: 25 min**

This vibrant salad combines the earthy flavors of kale with the satisfying crunch of roasted chickpeas, all brought together with a tangy lemon-tahini dressing. Perfect for a nutritious lunch or a light dinner.

### Equipment

Baking Sheet, Mixing Bowl, Whisk

### Ingredients

- 1 can (15 oz) chickpeas, drained and rinsed
- 1 tbsp olive oil
- 1 tsp smoked paprika
- 1/2 tsp garlic powder
- 1/4 tsp salt
- 8 oz kale, stems removed and leaves chopped
- 1/4 cup lemon juice
- 2 tbsp tahini
- 1 tbsp honey
- 1/4 cup water
- 1/4 cup sliced almonds, toasted

### Directions

1. Preheat the oven to 400°F (200°C).
2. Toss chickpeas with olive oil, smoked paprika, garlic powder, and salt. Spread on a baking sheet and roast for 20-25 minutes until crispy.
3. In a mixing bowl, whisk together lemon juice, tahini, honey, and water until smooth.
4. Massage the chopped kale with half of the dressing until well coated.
5. Top the kale with roasted chickpeas and toasted almonds. Drizzle with remaining dressing before serving.

### Nutritional Information

Calories: 210, Protein: 8g, Carbohydrates: 25g, Fat: 10g, Fiber: 6g, Cholesterol: 0mg, Sodium: 220mg, Potassium: 450mg

# MANGO & BLACK BEAN SUMMER SALAD

**Servings 4 | Prep: 15 min | Cook: 0 min**

This refreshing Mango & Black Bean Summer Salad combines the sweetness of ripe mangoes with the earthiness of black beans, creating a vibrant and nutritious dish perfect for warm days.

### Equipment

Mixing Bowl, Cutting Board, Knife

### Ingredients

- 1 cup diced mango
- 1 cup canned black beans, rinsed and drained
- 1 cup cherry tomatoes, halved
- 1/4 cup red onion, finely chopped
- 1/4 cup fresh cilantro, chopped
- 1 tbsp lime juice
- 1 tbsp olive oil
- 1/2 tsp salt
- 1/4 tsp black pepper

### Directions

1. In a mixing bowl, combine diced mango, black beans, cherry tomatoes, red onion, and cilantro.
2. In a small bowl, whisk together lime juice, olive oil, salt, and black pepper.
3. Pour the dressing over the salad ingredients.
4. Toss gently to combine, ensuring all ingredients are coated with the dressing.
5. Serve immediately or refrigerate for up to 2 hours to allow flavors to meld.

### Nutritional Information

Calories: 150, Protein: 4g, Carbohydrates: 28g, Fat: 4g, Fiber: 7g, Cholesterol: 0mg, Sodium: 300mg, Potassium: 450mg

# MEDITERRANEAN CUCUMBER & TOMATO SALAD

**Servings 4 | Prep: 15 min | Cook: 0 min**

This refreshing Mediterranean Cucumber & Tomato Salad is a vibrant mix of crisp cucumbers, juicy tomatoes, and tangy feta, perfect for a light and healthy meal.

### Equipment

Cutting Board, Knife, Large Mixing Bowl, Whisk

### Ingredients

- 2 cups diced cucumber
- 2 cups cherry tomatoes, halved
- 1/2 cup red onion, thinly sliced
- 1/4 cup Kalamata olives, pitted and sliced
- 1/4 cup crumbled feta cheese
- 2 tbsp extra-virgin olive oil
- 1 tbsp red wine vinegar
- 1 tsp dried oregano
- Salt and pepper to taste

### Directions

1. In a large mixing bowl, combine the diced cucumber, cherry tomatoes, red onion, and Kalamata olives.
2. In a small bowl, whisk together the olive oil, red wine vinegar, dried oregano, salt, and pepper.
3. Pour the dressing over the salad ingredients and toss gently to combine.
4. Sprinkle the crumbled feta cheese over the top of the salad.
5. Serve immediately or refrigerate for up to 2 hours to allow flavors to meld.

### Nutritional Information

Calories: 150, Protein: 3g, Carbohydrates: 10g, Fat: 11g, Fiber: 2g, Cholesterol: 10mg, Sodium: 250mg, Potassium: 350mg

# SPINACH & POMEGRANATE SUPERFOOD SALAD

**Servings 4 | Prep: 15 min | Cook: 0 min**

This vibrant salad combines fresh spinach with the sweet-tart burst of pomegranate seeds, offering a delightful mix of textures and flavors. It's a nutrient-packed dish perfect for a refreshing meal or side.

### Equipment

Mixing Bowl, Whisk, Salad Tongs

### Ingredients

- 6 oz fresh spinach leaves
- 1 cup pomegranate seeds
- 1/2 cup walnuts, toasted
- 1/4 cup feta cheese, crumbled
- 1/4 cup red onion, thinly sliced
- 2 tbsp extra-virgin olive oil
- 1 tbsp balsamic vinegar
- 1 tsp honey
- Salt and pepper to taste

### Directions

1. In a mixing bowl, whisk together olive oil, balsamic vinegar, honey, salt, and pepper to create the dressing.
2. In a large salad bowl, combine spinach, pomegranate seeds, walnuts, feta cheese, and red onion.
3. Drizzle the dressing over the salad ingredients.
4. Toss gently with salad tongs to ensure even coating.
5. Serve immediately and enjoy the fresh flavors.

### Nutritional Information

Calories: 210, Protein: 5g, Carbohydrates: 15g, Fat: 16g, Fiber: 4g, Cholesterol: 8mg, Sodium: 150mg, Potassium: 450mg

# ASIAN SESAME GINGER SLAW

**Servings 4 | Prep: 15 min | Cook: 0 min**

This vibrant Asian Sesame Ginger Slaw is a refreshing and crunchy salad, perfect for a light meal or as a side dish. The combination of fresh vegetables and a tangy sesame ginger dressing makes it irresistible.

### Equipment

Large Mixing Bowl, Whisk, Measuring Cups and Spoons

### Ingredients

- 3 cups shredded green cabbage
- 1 cup shredded red cabbage
- 1 cup shredded carrots
- 1/4 cup chopped green onions
- 1/4 cup chopped fresh cilantro
- 2 tbsp sesame seeds
- 1/4 cup rice vinegar
- 2 tbsp soy sauce (low sodium)
- 1 tbsp sesame oil
- 1 tbsp grated fresh ginger
- 1 tbsp honey
- 1 tsp garlic, minced

### Directions

1. In a large mixing bowl, combine the green cabbage, red cabbage, carrots, green onions, cilantro, and sesame seeds.
2. In a separate bowl, whisk together the rice vinegar, soy sauce, sesame oil, ginger, honey, and garlic until well combined.
3. Pour the dressing over the cabbage mixture and toss until the vegetables are evenly coated.
4. Let the slaw sit for at least 10 minutes to allow the flavors to meld.
5. Serve chilled or at room temperature.

### Nutritional Information

Calories: 120, Protein: 3g, Carbohydrates: 18g, Fat: 5g, Fiber: 4g, Cholesterol: 0mg, Sodium: 320mg, Potassium: 350mg

# ROASTED BEET & WALNUT SALAD

**Servings 4 | Prep: 15 min | Cook: 45 min**

This vibrant salad combines the earthy sweetness of roasted beets with the crunch of walnuts, all brought together by a tangy dressing. Perfect for a refreshing and nutritious meal.

### Equipment

Oven, Baking Sheet, Mixing Bowl

### Ingredients

- 1 lb beets, peeled and cut into wedges
- 2 tbsp olive oil
- 1/2 cup walnuts, roughly chopped
- 4 cups mixed greens
- 1/4 cup goat cheese, crumbled
- 2 tbsp balsamic vinegar
- Salt and pepper to taste

### Directions

1. Preheat the oven to 400°F (200°C).
2. Toss the beet wedges with 1 tbsp olive oil, salt, and pepper. Spread on a baking sheet and roast for 35-40 minutes, until tender.
3. In a dry skillet over medium heat, toast the walnuts for 3-4 minutes until fragrant.
4. In a mixing bowl, whisk together the remaining olive oil and balsamic vinegar. Season with salt and pepper.
5. In a large bowl, combine the roasted beets, mixed greens, walnuts, and goat cheese. Drizzle with the dressing and toss gently to combine.
6. Serve immediately, garnished with additional walnuts or cheese if desired.

### Nutritional Information

Calories: 210, Protein: 6g, Carbohydrates: 18g, Fat: 15g, Fiber: 4g, Cholesterol: 5mg, Sodium: 150mg, Potassium: 450mg

# LEMON GARLIC LENTIL SALAD

**Servings 4 | Prep: 15 min | Cook: 20 min**

This refreshing Lemon Garlic Lentil Salad is a delightful blend of earthy lentils, zesty lemon, and aromatic garlic, perfect for a light lunch or a side dish.

### Equipment

Medium Saucepan, Large Mixing Bowl, Whisk

### Ingredients

- 1 cup green lentils
- 3 cups water
- 1/4 cup fresh lemon juice
- 2 tablespoons olive oil
- 2 cloves garlic, minced
- 1/2 teaspoon salt
- 1/4 teaspoon black pepper
- 1/2 cup cherry tomatoes, halved
- 1/4 cup red onion, finely chopped
- 1/4 cup fresh parsley, chopped

### Directions

1. Rinse lentils under cold water. In a medium saucepan, combine lentils and water. Bring to a boil, then reduce heat and simmer for 20 minutes or until tender. Drain and let cool.
2. In a large mixing bowl, whisk together lemon juice, olive oil, garlic, salt, and black pepper.
3. Add cooled lentils, cherry tomatoes, red onion, and parsley to the bowl.
4. Toss gently to combine, ensuring the dressing coats all ingredients evenly.
5. Serve immediately or refrigerate for 30 minutes to allow flavors to meld.

### Nutritional Information

Calories: 210, Protein: 10g, Carbohydrates: 30g, Fat: 7g, Fiber: 12g, Cholesterol: 0mg, Sodium: 310mg, Potassium: 450mg

# GRILLED CHICKEN & AVOCADO BOWL

**Servings 4 | Prep: 15 min | Cook: 20 min**

This vibrant and nutritious bowl combines the smoky flavor of grilled chicken with the creamy texture of avocado, all atop a bed of fresh greens. Perfect for a wholesome lunch or dinner.

### Equipment

Grill Pan, Mixing Bowl, Tongs

### Ingredients

- 1 lb boneless, skinless chicken breasts
- 2 tbsp olive oil
- 1 tsp garlic powder
- 1 tsp paprika
- 1/2 tsp salt
- 1/4 tsp black pepper
- 2 ripe avocados, diced
- 4 cups mixed salad greens
- 1 cup cherry tomatoes, halved
- 1/4 cup red onion, thinly sliced
- 1 tbsp lemon juice

### Directions

1. Preheat the grill pan over medium-high heat.
2. In a mixing bowl, coat the chicken breasts with olive oil, garlic powder, paprika, salt, and black pepper.
3. Grill the chicken for 6-7 minutes on each side or until fully cooked. Remove from heat and let rest for 5 minutes before slicing.
4. In a large bowl, combine the salad greens, cherry tomatoes, red onion, and avocado.
5. Drizzle lemon juice over the salad mixture and toss gently.
6. Top the salad with sliced grilled chicken and serve immediately.

### Nutritional Information

Calories: 350, Protein: 30g, Carbohydrates: 12g, Fat: 20g, Fiber: 7g, Cholesterol: 70mg, Sodium: 300mg, Potassium: 900mg

# APPLE & WALNUT ARUGULA SALAD

**Servings 4 | Prep: 15 min | Cook: 0 min**

This refreshing salad combines the peppery taste of arugula with the sweetness of apples and the crunch of walnuts, all brought together with a light vinaigrette. Perfect for a quick, nutritious meal.

### Equipment

Salad Bowl, Whisk, Measuring Cups

### Ingredients

- 5 oz arugula
- 1 large apple, thinly sliced
- 1/2 cup walnuts, toasted
- 1/4 cup crumbled feta cheese
- 2 tbsp extra-virgin olive oil
- 1 tbsp apple cider vinegar
- 1 tsp honey
- Salt and pepper to taste

### Directions

1. In a large salad bowl, combine arugula, apple slices, and toasted walnuts.
2. In a small bowl, whisk together olive oil, apple cider vinegar, honey, salt, and pepper to create the dressing.
3. Drizzle the dressing over the salad and toss gently to combine.
4. Sprinkle crumbled feta cheese on top before serving.
5. Serve immediately and enjoy the fresh flavors.

### Nutritional Information

Calories: 210, Protein: 4g, Carbohydrates: 14g, Fat: 17g, Fiber: 3g, Cholesterol: 8mg, Sodium: 120mg, Potassium: 220mg

# ZESTY QUINOA & CRANBERRY SALAD

**Servings 4 | Prep: 15 min | Cook: 15 min**

A refreshing and vibrant salad that combines the nutty flavor of quinoa with the tartness of cranberries, perfect for a light lunch or a side dish.

### Equipment

Medium Saucepan, Large Mixing Bowl, Whisk

### Ingredients

- 1 cup quinoa
- 2 cups water
- 1/2 cup dried cranberries
- 1/4 cup chopped fresh parsley
- 1/4 cup chopped almonds
- 1/4 cup diced red onion
- 1/4 cup fresh lemon juice
- 2 tablespoons olive oil
- 1 teaspoon honey
- Salt and pepper to taste

### Directions

1. Rinse quinoa under cold water. In a medium saucepan, combine quinoa and water. Bring to a boil, then reduce heat to low, cover, and simmer for 15 minutes or until water is absorbed.
2. In a large mixing bowl, combine cooked quinoa, cranberries, parsley, almonds, and red onion.
3. In a small bowl, whisk together lemon juice, olive oil, honey, salt, and pepper.
4. Pour the dressing over the quinoa mixture and toss to combine.
5. Serve immediately or refrigerate for 30 minutes to allow flavors to meld.

### Nutritional Information

Calories: 280, Protein: 6g, Carbohydrates: 42g, Fat: 10g, Fiber: 5g, Cholesterol: 0mg, Sodium: 10mg, Potassium: 320mg

# RAINBOW VEGGIE NOODLE SALAD

**Servings 4 | Prep: 20 min | Cook: 0 min**

This vibrant and refreshing salad combines colorful veggie noodles with a zesty dressing, perfect for a light lunch or a side dish.

### Equipment

Spiralizer, Large Mixing Bowl, Whisk

### Ingredients

- 1 medium zucchini, spiralized
- 1 medium carrot, spiralized
- 1 red bell pepper, thinly sliced
- 1 cup red cabbage, thinly sliced
- 1/2 cup cherry tomatoes, halved
- 1/4 cup fresh cilantro, chopped
- 2 tbsp olive oil
- 1 tbsp apple cider vinegar
- 1 tbsp lemon juice
- 1 tsp honey
- 1/2 tsp salt
- 1/4 tsp black pepper

### Directions

1. Spiralize the zucchini and carrot, and place them in a large mixing bowl.
2. Add the sliced red bell pepper, red cabbage, cherry tomatoes, and cilantro to the bowl.
3. In a small bowl, whisk together olive oil, apple cider vinegar, lemon juice, honey, salt, and black pepper to create the dressing.
4. Pour the dressing over the veggie noodles and toss gently to combine.
5. Serve immediately or refrigerate for up to 2 hours to allow flavors to meld.

### Nutritional Information

Calories: 120, Protein: 2g, Carbohydrates: 12g, Fat: 8g, Fiber: 3g, Cholesterol: 0mg, Sodium: 200mg, Potassium: 450mg

# AVOCADO & ROASTED SWEET POTATO SALAD

**Servings 4 | Prep: 15 min | Cook: 25 min**

This vibrant salad combines creamy avocado with the natural sweetness of roasted sweet potatoes, creating a delightful balance of flavors and textures. Perfect for a nutritious lunch or a refreshing side dish.

### Equipment

Baking Sheet, Mixing Bowl, Whisk

### Ingredients

- 2 medium sweet potatoes, peeled and cubed (about 1 lb)
- 2 tbsp olive oil
- 1 tsp ground cumin
- 1/2 tsp salt
- 1/4 tsp black pepper
- 2 ripe avocados, diced
- 4 cups mixed greens
- 1/4 cup red onion, thinly sliced
- 1/4 cup fresh cilantro, chopped
- 2 tbsp lime juice
- 1 tbsp honey

### Directions

1. Preheat the oven to 400°F (200°C). Toss the sweet potato cubes with olive oil, cumin, salt, and pepper. Spread evenly on a baking sheet.
2. Roast in the oven for 20-25 minutes, or until tender and slightly caramelized. Allow to cool slightly.
3. In a large mixing bowl, combine the roasted sweet potatoes, diced avocados, mixed greens, red onion, and cilantro.
4. In a small bowl, whisk together lime juice and honey. Drizzle over the salad and gently toss to combine.
5. Serve immediately, garnished with additional cilantro if desired.

### Nutritional Information

Calories: 320, Protein: 4g, Carbohydrates: 42g, Fat: 18g, Fiber: 10g, Cholesterol: 0mg, Sodium: 250mg, Potassium: 980mg

# CLASSIC GREEK SALAD WITH A TWIST

**Servings 4 | Prep: 15 min | Cook: 0 min**

This refreshing Greek salad combines traditional flavors with a modern twist, adding a burst of color and nutrients to your meal. Perfect for a light lunch or a vibrant side dish.

### Equipment

Mixing Bowl, Whisk, Cutting Board, Knife

### Ingredients

- 2 cups chopped romaine lettuce
- 1 cup cherry tomatoes, halved
- 1 cup cucumber, diced
- 1/2 cup red onion, thinly sliced
- 1/2 cup Kalamata olives, pitted and halved
- 1/2 cup feta cheese, crumbled
- 1/4 cup fresh mint leaves, chopped
- 1/4 cup extra-virgin olive oil
- 2 tbsp red wine vinegar
- 1 tsp dried oregano
- 1/2 tsp garlic powder
- Salt and pepper to taste

### Directions

1. In a large mixing bowl, combine the romaine lettuce, cherry tomatoes, cucumber, red onion, and Kalamata olives.
2. Add the crumbled feta cheese and chopped mint leaves to the salad mixture.
3. In a small bowl, whisk together the olive oil, red wine vinegar, dried oregano, garlic powder, salt, and pepper to create the dressing.
4. Pour the dressing over the salad and toss gently to combine all ingredients evenly.
5. Serve immediately or refrigerate for up to 30 minutes to allow flavors to meld.

### Nutritional Information

Calories: 210, Protein: 5g, Carbohydrates: 10g, Fat: 18g, Fiber: 3g, Cholesterol: 15mg, Sodium: 450mg, Potassium: 350mg

# CABBAGE & CARROT DETOX SALAD

**Servings 4 | Prep: 15 min | Cook: 0 min**

This vibrant and refreshing detox salad combines the crunch of cabbage and carrots with a zesty dressing, perfect for a clean eating lifestyle.

### Equipment

Mixing Bowl, Whisk, Grater

### Ingredients

- 2 cups shredded green cabbage
- 1 cup shredded carrots
- 1/4 cup chopped fresh cilantro
- 1/4 cup fresh lemon juice
- 2 tablespoons olive oil
- 1 tablespoon apple cider vinegar
- 1 teaspoon honey
- 1/2 teaspoon salt
- 1/4 teaspoon black pepper

### Directions

1. In a large mixing bowl, combine the shredded cabbage, shredded carrots, and chopped cilantro.
2. In a separate small bowl, whisk together the lemon juice, olive oil, apple cider vinegar, honey, salt, and black pepper until well combined.
3. Pour the dressing over the cabbage mixture and toss until the salad is evenly coated.
4. Let the salad sit for 5 minutes to allow the flavors to meld.
5. Serve immediately or refrigerate for up to 2 hours for a chilled option.

### Nutritional Information

Calories: 110, Protein: 1g, Carbohydrates: 10g, Fat: 8g, Fiber: 3g, Cholesterol: 0mg, Sodium: 300mg, Potassium: 250mg

# TURMERIC & GINGER DRESSING

**Servings 4 | Prep: 10 min | Cook: 0 min**

This vibrant and zesty dressing combines the earthy warmth of turmeric with the zing of fresh ginger, perfect for elevating any salad with a burst of flavor and health benefits.

### Equipment

Blender, Measuring Cups, Measuring Spoons

### Ingredients

- 1/4 cup extra-virgin olive oil
- 2 tbsp apple cider vinegar
- 1 tbsp fresh lemon juice
- 1 tbsp honey
- 1 tsp ground turmeric
- 1 tsp fresh ginger, grated
- 1/2 tsp garlic powder
- 1/4 tsp sea salt
- 1/4 tsp black pepper

### Directions

1. In a blender, combine the olive oil, apple cider vinegar, and lemon juice.
2. Add the honey, ground turmeric, and grated ginger to the blender.
3. Sprinkle in the garlic powder, sea salt, and black pepper.
4. Blend on high speed until the mixture is smooth and well combined.
5. Taste and adjust seasoning if necessary.
6. Transfer the dressing to a jar or bottle for easy pouring.
7. Store in the refrigerator for up to one week and shake well before each use.

### Nutritional Information

Calories: 120, Protein: 0g, Carbohydrates: 5g, Fat: 12g, Fiber: 0g, Cholesterol: 0mg, Sodium: 150mg, Potassium: 30mg

## HOMEMADE HONEY MUSTARD DRESSING

**Servings 8 | Prep: 10 min | Cook: 0 min**

This tangy and sweet homemade honey mustard dressing is perfect for drizzling over salads or as a dip for fresh veggies. Made with simple, clean ingredients, it adds a burst of flavor to any dish.

### Equipment

Mixing Bowl, Whisk, Measuring Spoons

### Ingredients

- 1/2 cup Dijon mustard
- 1/4 cup honey
- 2 tablespoons apple cider vinegar
- 1/4 cup extra-virgin olive oil
- 1/4 teaspoon garlic powder
- 1/4 teaspoon salt
- 1/8 teaspoon black pepper

### Directions

1. In a mixing bowl, combine the Dijon mustard and honey. Whisk until smooth.
2. Add the apple cider vinegar and whisk again to incorporate.
3. Slowly drizzle in the olive oil while continuously whisking to emulsify the dressing.
4. Stir in the garlic powder, salt, and black pepper. Adjust seasoning to taste.
5. Transfer the dressing to a jar or bottle for easy storage. Shake well before each use.

### Nutritional Information

Calories: 110, Protein: 0g, Carbohydrates: 8g, Fat: 9g, Fiber: 0g, Cholesterol: 0mg, Sodium: 150mg, Potassium: 10mg

## CILANTRO LIME VINAIGRETTE

**Servings 8 | Prep: 10 min | Cook: 0 min**

This vibrant and zesty cilantro lime vinaigrette is perfect for drizzling over salads or as a marinade for grilled proteins. Its fresh and tangy flavors will elevate any dish with a burst of citrus and herbaceous notes.

### Equipment

Blender, Measuring Cups, Measuring Spoons

### Ingredients

- 1 cup fresh cilantro leaves, packed
- 1/2 cup extra virgin olive oil
- 1/4 cup fresh lime juice
- 1 tablespoon honey
- 1 teaspoon Dijon mustard
- 1 clove garlic, minced
- 1/2 teaspoon sea salt
- 1/4 teaspoon black pepper

### Directions

1. Combine cilantro leaves, olive oil, lime juice, honey, Dijon mustard, and minced garlic in a blender.
2. Blend on high speed until the mixture is smooth and emulsified.
3. Season with sea salt and black pepper to taste.
4. Blend again briefly to ensure all ingredients are well incorporated.
5. Transfer the vinaigrette to a jar or bottle for storage.
6. Shake well before each use to maintain consistency.

### Nutritional Information

Calories: 100, Protein: 0g, Carbohydrates: 2g, Fat: 11g, Fiber: 0g, Cholesterol: 0mg, Sodium: 75mg, Potassium: 30mg

## CREAMY TAHINI DRESSING

**Servings 4 | Prep: 10 min | Cook: 0 min**

This creamy tahini dressing is a versatile and delicious addition to any salad, offering a nutty flavor with a hint of lemon and garlic. Perfect for those who love a rich, yet healthy dressing.

### Equipment

Mixing Bowl, Whisk, Measuring Cups and Spoons

### Ingredients

- 1/2 cup tahini
- 1/4 cup water
- 2 tbsp lemon juice
- 1 tbsp olive oil
- 1 tbsp apple cider vinegar
- 1 clove garlic, minced
- 1 tsp maple syrup
- 1/2 tsp salt
- 1/4 tsp black pepper

### Directions

1. In a mixing bowl, combine tahini and water, whisking until smooth.
2. Add lemon juice, olive oil, and apple cider vinegar; mix well.
3. Stir in minced garlic, maple syrup, salt, and black pepper.
4. Whisk all ingredients together until the dressing is creamy and well-blended.
5. Adjust seasoning to taste, adding more lemon juice or salt if desired.

### Nutritional Information

Calories: 160, Protein: 4g, Carbohydrates: 7g, Fat: 14g, Fiber: 3g, Cholesterol: 0mg, Sodium: 300mg, Potassium: 120mg

## MAPLE BALSAMIC DRESSING

**Servings 8 | Prep: 5 min | Cook: 0 min**

This Maple Balsamic Dressing is a perfect blend of sweet and tangy flavors, ideal for drizzling over fresh greens or roasted vegetables.

### Equipment

Whisk, Mixing Bowl, Measuring Spoons

### Ingredients

- 1/2 cup balsamic vinegar
- 1/4 cup pure maple syrup
- 1/4 cup extra-virgin olive oil
- 1 tablespoon Dijon mustard
- 1/2 teaspoon garlic powder
- Salt and freshly ground black pepper to taste

### Directions

1. In a mixing bowl, combine balsamic vinegar and pure maple syrup.
2. Add extra-virgin olive oil and Dijon mustard to the mixture.
3. Sprinkle in garlic powder, then season with salt and freshly ground black pepper to taste.
4. Whisk all ingredients together until well combined and emulsified.
5. Taste and adjust seasoning if necessary.
6. Transfer the dressing to a jar or bottle for easy storage and shake well before each use.

### Nutritional Information

Calories: 80, Protein: 0g, Carbohydrates: 7g, Fat: 6g, Fiber: 0g, Cholesterol: 0mg, Sodium: 40mg, Potassium: 20mg

## SPICY MANGO DRESSING

**Servings 4 | Prep: 10 min | Cook: 0 min**

This vibrant and zesty Spicy Mango Dressing adds a tropical twist to your salads, combining the sweetness of ripe mangoes with a hint of heat for a refreshing and flavorful experience.

### Equipment

Blender, Measuring Cups, Measuring Spoons

### Ingredients

- 1 cup ripe mango, peeled and diced
- 2 tbsp lime juice
- 1 tbsp apple cider vinegar
- 1 tbsp honey
- 1 tsp chili flakes
- 1/4 cup olive oil
- 1/4 tsp salt
- 1/8 tsp black pepper

### Directions

1. Combine mango, lime juice, apple cider vinegar, honey, and chili flakes in a blender.
2. Blend until smooth and creamy.
3. Gradually add olive oil while blending to emulsify the dressing.
4. Season with salt and black pepper to taste.
5. Transfer to a jar and refrigerate for at least 30 minutes before serving to enhance flavors.

### Nutritional Information

Calories: 120, Protein: 0.5g, Carbohydrates: 15g, Fat: 8g, Fiber: 1g, Cholesterol: 0mg, Sodium: 150mg, Potassium: 120mg

## VEGAN RANCH DRESSING

**Servings 8 | Prep: 10 min | Cook: 0 min**

This creamy Vegan Ranch Dressing is a delightful, dairy-free alternative to the classic favorite. Perfect for salads, dipping, or drizzling over your favorite dishes, it combines the tanginess of lemon with the richness of cashews for a guilt-free indulgence.

### Equipment

Blender, Measuring Cups, Measuring Spoons

### Ingredients

- 1 cup raw cashews, soaked
- 3/4 cup water
- 2 tablespoons lemon juice
- 1 tablespoon apple cider vinegar
- 1 tablespoon olive oil
- 1 teaspoon garlic powder
- 1 teaspoon onion powder
- 1/2 teaspoon dried dill
- 1/2 teaspoon salt
- 1/4 teaspoon black pepper
- 2 tablespoons fresh parsley, chopped

### Directions

1. Soak the cashews in water for at least 2 hours or overnight, then drain.
2. In a blender, combine the soaked cashews, water, lemon juice, apple cider vinegar, and olive oil. Blend until smooth and creamy.
3. Add the garlic powder, onion powder, dried dill, salt, and black pepper to the blender. Blend again until well combined.
4. Stir in the chopped fresh parsley.
5. Adjust seasoning to taste and add more water if a thinner consistency is desired.
6. Transfer to a jar and refrigerate for at least 30 minutes before serving to enhance flavors.

### Nutritional Information

Calories: 90, Protein: 3g, Carbohydrates: 7g, Fat: 6g, Fiber: 1g, Cholesterol: 0mg, Sodium: 150mg, Potassium: 125mg

# GARLIC & LEMON YOGURT DRESSING

**Servings 4 | Prep: 10 min | Cook: 0 min**

This refreshing Garlic & Lemon Yogurt Dressing is a zesty and creamy addition to any salad, offering a burst of flavor with every bite.

### Equipment

Mixing Bowl, Whisk, Measuring Spoons

### Ingredients

- 1 cup plain Greek yogurt
- 2 tbsp fresh lemon juice
- 1 tbsp olive oil
- 2 cloves garlic, minced
- 1 tsp honey
- 1/2 tsp salt
- 1/4 tsp black pepper
- 1 tbsp fresh dill, chopped (optional)

### Directions

1. In a mixing bowl, combine the Greek yogurt, lemon juice, and olive oil.
2. Add the minced garlic, honey, salt, and black pepper.
3. Whisk the ingredients together until smooth and well combined.
4. Stir in the fresh dill if using, for an extra burst of flavor.
5. Taste and adjust seasoning if necessary.
6. Serve immediately or refrigerate for up to 3 days.

### Nutritional Information

Calories: 70, Protein: 4g, Carbohydrates: 5g, Fat: 4g, Fiber: 0g, Cholesterol: 5mg, Sodium: 220mg, Potassium: 150mg

# ROASTED RED PEPPER DRESSING

**Servings 8 | Prep: 10 min | Cook: 5 min**

This vibrant and flavorful dressing combines the smoky sweetness of roasted red peppers with tangy vinegar and aromatic herbs, perfect for drizzling over salads or as a dip for fresh veggies.

### Equipment

Blender, Measuring Cups, Measuring Spoons

### Ingredients

- 1 cup roasted red peppers, drained
- 2 tablespoons olive oil
- 2 tablespoons apple cider vinegar
- 1 tablespoon lemon juice
- 1 teaspoon honey
- 1 clove garlic, minced
- 1/2 teaspoon salt
- 1/4 teaspoon black pepper
- 1/4 teaspoon dried oregano

### Directions

1. Combine roasted red peppers, olive oil, apple cider vinegar, lemon juice, honey, and minced garlic in a blender.
2. Blend until smooth and creamy.
3. Add salt, black pepper, and dried oregano. Blend again until well combined.
4. Taste and adjust seasoning if necessary.
5. Transfer to a jar or bottle and refrigerate for at least 30 minutes before serving to allow flavors to meld.

### Nutritional Information

Calories: 35, Protein: 0.5g, Carbohydrates: 2g, Fat: 3g, Fiber: 0.5g, Cholesterol: 0mg, Sodium: 150mg, Potassium: 50mg

# RASPBERRY VINAIGRETTE

**Servings 6 | Prep: 10 min | Cook: 0 min**

This vibrant and tangy raspberry vinaigrette is perfect for drizzling over fresh greens. Its sweet and tart flavor profile adds a refreshing twist to any salad.

### Equipment

Blender, Measuring Cups, Measuring Spoons

### Ingredients

- 1 cup fresh raspberries
- 1/4 cup apple cider vinegar
- 1/4 cup extra-virgin olive oil
- 2 tbsp honey
- 1 tsp Dijon mustard
- 1/4 tsp salt
- 1/4 tsp black pepper

### Directions

1. Combine raspberries and apple cider vinegar in a blender.
2. Blend until smooth, then strain through a fine mesh sieve to remove seeds.
3. Return the strained mixture to the blender.
4. Add olive oil, honey, Dijon mustard, salt, and black pepper.
5. Blend until fully emulsified and smooth.
6. Taste and adjust seasoning if necessary.
7. Store in a sealed container in the refrigerator for up to one week.

### Nutritional Information

Calories: 90, Protein: 0g, Carbohydrates: 7g, Fat: 7g, Fiber: 1g, Cholesterol: 0mg, Sodium: 100mg, Potassium: 60mg

# GINGER MISO DRESSING

**Servings 4 | Prep: 10 min | Cook: 0 min**

This Ginger Miso Dressing is a delightful blend of savory and tangy flavors, perfect for elevating any salad with its rich umami taste and zesty ginger kick.

### Equipment

Blender, Measuring Cups, Measuring Spoons

### Ingredients

- 1/4 cup white miso paste
- 2 tbsp fresh ginger, grated
- 2 tbsp rice vinegar
- 2 tbsp soy sauce
- 1 tbsp honey
- 1/4 cup sesame oil
- 2 tbsp water

### Directions

1. Combine the miso paste, grated ginger, rice vinegar, soy sauce, and honey in a blender.
2. Blend on low speed until the mixture is smooth.
3. Gradually add the sesame oil while blending to emulsify the dressing.
4. Add water to achieve desired consistency and blend again briefly.
5. Taste and adjust seasoning if necessary.
6. Transfer to a jar and refrigerate until ready to use.

### Nutritional Information

Calories: 150, Protein: 2g, Carbohydrates: 10g, Fat: 12g, Fiber: 1g, Cholesterol: 0mg, Sodium: 600mg, Potassium: 100mg

# Soups & Stews

## CARROT GINGER DETOX SOUP

**Servings 4 | Prep: 10 min | Cook: 25 min**

This vibrant and nourishing Carrot Ginger Detox Soup is perfect for a refreshing cleanse. With its warming ginger and sweet carrots, it's both comforting and invigorating.

### Equipment

Large Pot, Blender or Immersion Blender, Cutting Board

### Ingredients

- 1 tbsp olive oil
- 1 medium onion, chopped
- 1 lb carrots, peeled and sliced
- 1 tbsp fresh ginger, grated
- 4 cups vegetable broth
- 1 cup coconut milk
- 1 tsp salt
- 1/2 tsp black pepper
- 2 tbsp fresh lemon juice

### Directions

1. Heat olive oil in a large pot over medium heat. Add chopped onion and sauté until translucent.
2. Stir in carrots and ginger, cooking for about 5 minutes until carrots begin to soften.
3. Pour in vegetable broth, bringing the mixture to a boil. Reduce heat and simmer for 15 minutes.
4. Remove from heat and blend the soup until smooth using a blender or immersion blender.
5. Stir in coconut milk, salt, pepper, and lemon juice. Heat gently until warmed through.
6. Serve hot, garnished with fresh herbs if desired.

### Nutritional Information

Calories: 180, Protein: 3g, Carbohydrates: 22g, Fat: 10g, Fiber: 5g, Cholesterol: 0mg, Sodium: 600mg, Potassium: 650mg

## ROASTED TOMATO & BASIL SOUP

**Servings 4 | Prep: 10 min | Cook: 40 min**

This vibrant and flavorful soup captures the essence of fresh tomatoes and aromatic basil, perfect for a comforting and healthy meal.

### Equipment

Baking Sheet, Blender, Large Pot

### Ingredients

- 2 lbs ripe tomatoes, halved
- 1 medium onion, quartered
- 4 cloves garlic, peeled
- 2 tbsp olive oil
- 4 cups vegetable broth
- 1 cup fresh basil leaves
- Salt and pepper to taste

### Directions

1. Preheat the oven to 400°F (200°C).
2. Arrange the tomatoes, onion, and garlic on a baking sheet. Drizzle with olive oil and season with salt and pepper.
3. Roast in the oven for 25-30 minutes until the tomatoes are soft and slightly charred.
4. Transfer the roasted vegetables to a blender. Add the vegetable broth and blend until smooth.
5. Pour the mixture into a large pot and bring to a simmer over medium heat. Stir in the fresh basil leaves.
6. Simmer for 5-10 minutes to allow flavors to meld. Adjust seasoning with salt and pepper as needed.
7. Serve hot, garnished with additional basil leaves if desired.

### Nutritional Information

Calories: 180, Protein: 4g, Carbohydrates: 24g, Fat: 9g, Fiber: 6g, Cholesterol: 0mg, Sodium: 600mg, Potassium: 950mg

# SWEET POTATO & COCONUT SOUP

**Servings 4 | Prep: 15 min | Cook: 30 min**

This creamy and aromatic soup combines the natural sweetness of sweet potatoes with the rich, tropical flavor of coconut milk, creating a comforting and nourishing dish perfect for any season.

### Equipment

Large Pot, Blender, Wooden Spoon

### Ingredients

- 2 lbs sweet potatoes, peeled and cubed
- 1 tbsp olive oil
- 1 medium onion, chopped
- 2 cloves garlic, minced
- 1 tsp ground ginger
- 4 cups vegetable broth
- 1 cup coconut milk
- Salt and pepper to taste
- 2 tbsp fresh cilantro, chopped (for garnish)

### Directions

1. Heat olive oil in a large pot over medium heat. Add onion and garlic, sauté until onion is translucent.
2. Stir in ground ginger and cook for another minute until fragrant.
3. Add sweet potatoes and vegetable broth. Bring to a boil, then reduce heat and simmer until sweet potatoes are tender, about 20 minutes.
4. Remove from heat and carefully blend the soup until smooth using a blender.
5. Return the soup to the pot, stir in coconut milk, and season with salt and pepper. Heat through without boiling.
6. Serve hot, garnished with fresh cilantro.

### Nutritional Information

Calories: 280, Protein: 4g, Carbohydrates: 45g, Fat: 12g, Fiber: 7g, Cholesterol: 0 mg, Sodium: 400 mg, Potassium: 800 mg

# BUTTERNUT SQUASH & APPLE SOUP

**Servings 4 | Prep: 15 min | Cook: 30 min**

This delightful soup combines the natural sweetness of butternut squash and apples, creating a comforting and nutritious dish perfect for any season.

### Equipment

Large Pot, Blender, Knife

### Ingredients

- 2 lbs butternut squash, peeled and cubed
- 2 medium apples, peeled, cored, and chopped
- 1 medium onion, chopped
- 2 tbsp olive oil
- 4 cups vegetable broth
- 1 tsp ground cinnamon
- 1/2 tsp ground nutmeg
- Salt and pepper to taste

### Directions

1. Heat olive oil in a large pot over medium heat. Add onion and sauté until translucent.
2. Add butternut squash and apples to the pot, stirring occasionally for about 5 minutes.
3. Pour in the vegetable broth, then add cinnamon and nutmeg. Bring to a boil, then reduce heat and simmer for 20 minutes, or until squash is tender.
4. Carefully transfer the mixture to a blender and blend until smooth. Return to the pot and season with salt and pepper to taste.
5. Reheat the soup gently before serving.

### Nutritional Information

Calories: 180, Protein: 3g, Carbohydrates: 38g, Fat: 5g, Fiber: 7g, Cholesterol: 0 mg, Sodium: 450 mg, Potassium: 800 mg

# SPICED LENTIL & KALE SOUP

**Servings 4 | Prep: 15 min | Cook: 30 min**

This hearty and nourishing soup combines the earthy flavors of lentils with the vibrant freshness of kale, enhanced by a blend of warming spices. Perfect for a cozy, clean-eating meal.

### Equipment

Large Pot, Wooden Spoon, Measuring Cups and Spoons

### Ingredients

- 1 tbsp olive oil
- 1 medium onion, diced
- 2 cloves garlic, minced
- 1 tsp ground cumin
- 1/2 tsp ground coriander
- 1/4 tsp cayenne pepper (optional)
- 1 cup dried lentils, rinsed
- 6 cups vegetable broth
- 2 cups kale, chopped
- 1 medium carrot, diced
- Salt and pepper to taste
- 1 tbsp lemon juice

### Directions

1. Heat olive oil in a large pot over medium heat. Add onion and garlic, sauté until onion is translucent.
2. Stir in cumin, coriander, and cayenne pepper, cooking for 1 minute until fragrant.
3. Add lentils and vegetable broth. Bring to a boil, then reduce heat and simmer for 20 minutes.
4. Add kale and carrot, continue to simmer for another 10 minutes until lentils and vegetables are tender.
5. Season with salt, pepper, and lemon juice. Stir well and serve hot.

### Nutritional Information

Calories: 220, Protein: 12g, Carbohydrates: 35g, Fat: 5g, Fiber: 12g, Cholesterol: 0mg, Sodium: 600mg, Potassium: 500mg

# QUINOA & VEGETABLE BROTH BOWL

**Servings 4 | Prep: 15 min | Cook: 25 min**

A nourishing and hearty bowl filled with the goodness of quinoa and a medley of fresh vegetables, perfect for a wholesome meal.

### Equipment

Large Pot, Cutting Board, Knife

### Ingredients

- 1 cup quinoa, rinsed
- 2 tablespoons olive oil
- 1 medium onion, diced
- 2 cloves garlic, minced
- 1 cup carrots, sliced
- 1 cup zucchini, diced
- 1 cup broccoli florets
- 6 cups vegetable broth
- 1 teaspoon dried thyme
- Salt and pepper to taste
- 2 tablespoons fresh parsley, chopped

### Directions

1. Heat olive oil in a large pot over medium heat. Add onion and garlic, sauté until translucent.
2. Stir in carrots, zucchini, and broccoli, cooking for 5 minutes until slightly tender.
3. Add quinoa and vegetable broth to the pot, bringing to a boil.
4. Reduce heat, add thyme, salt, and pepper, and simmer for 15 minutes until quinoa is cooked.
5. Garnish with fresh parsley before serving.

### Nutritional Information

Calories: 220, Protein: 7g, Carbohydrates: 35g, Fat: 7g, Fiber: 6g, Cholesterol: 0mg, Sodium: 480mg, Potassium: 550mg

# CREAMY CAULIFLOWER & GARLIC SOUP

**Servings 4 | Prep: 10 min | Cook: 30 min**

This velvety soup combines the subtle sweetness of cauliflower with the rich aroma of roasted garlic, offering a comforting and nutritious meal perfect for any season.

### Equipment

Large Pot, Blender, Baking Sheet

### Ingredients

- 1 large head of cauliflower, cut into florets (about 2 lbs)
- 1 tablespoon olive oil
- 1 medium onion, chopped
- 4 cloves garlic, peeled
- 4 cups vegetable broth
- 1 cup unsweetened almond milk
- 1 teaspoon salt
- 1/2 teaspoon black pepper
- 1 tablespoon fresh lemon juice

### Directions

1. Preheat the oven to 400°F. Toss cauliflower florets and garlic cloves with olive oil, and spread them on a baking sheet. Roast for 20 minutes until tender and slightly golden.
2. In a large pot, sauté the chopped onion over medium heat until translucent, about 5 minutes.
3. Add the roasted cauliflower and garlic to the pot, then pour in the vegetable broth. Bring to a boil, then reduce heat and simmer for 10 minutes.
4. Remove from heat and carefully transfer the soup to a blender. Blend until smooth and creamy.
5. Return the soup to the pot, stir in almond milk, salt, pepper, and lemon juice. Heat gently until warmed through.
6. Adjust seasoning to taste and serve hot.

### Nutritional Information

Calories: 120, Protein: 5g, Carbohydrates: 18g, Fat: 4g, Fiber: 5g, Cholesterol: 0mg, Sodium: 600mg, Potassium: 500mg

# TURMERIC & LEMON CHICKPEA SOUP

**Servings 4 | Prep: 10 min | Cook: 25 min**

This vibrant and nourishing soup combines the earthy warmth of turmeric with the zesty brightness of lemon, creating a comforting dish that's both hearty and refreshing.

### Equipment

Large Pot, Wooden Spoon, Ladle

### Ingredients

- 1 tbsp olive oil
- 1 medium onion, diced
- 2 cloves garlic, minced
- 1 tsp ground turmeric
- 1/2 tsp ground cumin
- 4 cups vegetable broth
- 2 cups cooked chickpeas (or 1 can, drained and rinsed)
- 1 cup diced carrots
- 1/2 cup diced celery
- Juice of 1 lemon
- Salt and pepper to taste
- 1/4 cup chopped fresh parsley

### Directions

1. Heat olive oil in a large pot over medium heat. Add onion and garlic; sauté until onion is translucent.
2. Stir in turmeric and cumin; cook for 1 minute until fragrant.
3. Add vegetable broth, chickpeas, carrots, and celery. Bring to a boil, then reduce heat and simmer for 20 minutes.
4. Stir in lemon juice, salt, and pepper. Adjust seasoning as needed.
5. Serve hot, garnished with fresh parsley.

### Nutritional Information

Calories: 210, Protein: 8g, Carbohydrates: 32g, Fat: 6g, Fiber: 8g, Cholesterol: 0 mg, Sodium: 480 mg, Potassium: 420 mg

# HEARTY MUSHROOM & BARLEY STEW

**Servings 4 | Prep: 15 min | Cook: 45 min**

This comforting stew combines earthy mushrooms with wholesome barley, creating a nourishing and satisfying dish perfect for any season.

### Equipment

Large Pot, Wooden Spoon, Knife

### Ingredients

- 1 tbsp olive oil
- 1 medium onion, diced
- 2 cloves garlic, minced
- 8 oz mushrooms, sliced
- 1 cup carrots, diced
- 1 cup celery, diced
- 1 cup pearl barley
- 6 cups vegetable broth
- 1 tsp dried thyme
- Salt and pepper to taste
- 2 tbsp fresh parsley, chopped

### Directions

1. Heat olive oil in a large pot over medium heat. Add onion and garlic, sauté until onion is translucent.
2. Add mushrooms, carrots, and celery. Cook for about 5 minutes until vegetables begin to soften.
3. Stir in barley, vegetable broth, and thyme. Bring to a boil, then reduce heat to low and cover.
4. Simmer for 35-40 minutes, or until barley is tender. Stir occasionally.
5. Season with salt and pepper to taste. Garnish with fresh parsley before serving.

### Nutritional Information

Calories: 250, Protein: 8g, Carbohydrates: 45g, Fat: 5g, Fiber: 8g, Cholesterol: 0mg, Sodium: 600mg, Potassium: 500mg

# MOROCCAN SPICED CARROT SOUP

**Servings 4 | Prep: 15 min | Cook: 30 min**

This vibrant Moroccan Spiced Carrot Soup is a delightful blend of sweet and savory flavors, enhanced by warm spices. Perfect for a cozy meal, it's both nourishing and satisfying.

### Equipment

Large Pot, Blender, Wooden Spoon

### Ingredients

- 1 tbsp olive oil
- 1 medium onion, chopped
- 2 lbs carrots, peeled and sliced
- 2 tsp ground cumin
- 1 tsp ground coriander
- 1/2 tsp ground cinnamon
- 4 cups vegetable broth
- 1 cup coconut milk
- Salt and pepper to taste
- 2 tbsp fresh cilantro, chopped (for garnish)

### Directions

1. Heat olive oil in a large pot over medium heat. Add onion and sauté until translucent.
2. Stir in carrots, cumin, coriander, and cinnamon. Cook for 5 minutes, stirring occasionally.
3. Pour in vegetable broth, bring to a boil, then reduce heat and simmer until carrots are tender, about 20 minutes.
4. Remove from heat and blend the soup until smooth using a blender. Return to pot.
5. Stir in coconut milk, season with salt and pepper, and heat through.
6. Serve hot, garnished with fresh cilantro.

### Nutritional Information

Calories: 210, Protein: 3g, Carbohydrates: 28g, Fat: 11g, Fiber: 6g, Cholesterol: 0 mg, Sodium: 480 mg, Potassium: 800 mg

# ROASTED RED PEPPER & QUINOA SOUP

**Servings 4 | Prep: 15 min | Cook: 30 min**

This vibrant and hearty soup combines the smoky sweetness of roasted red peppers with the nutty texture of quinoa, creating a nourishing and flavorful dish perfect for any season.

### Equipment

Blender, Large Pot, Baking Sheet

### Ingredients

- 4 large red bell peppers
- 1 cup quinoa, rinsed
- 1 tablespoon olive oil
- 1 medium onion, chopped
- 2 cloves garlic, minced
- 4 cups vegetable broth
- 1 teaspoon smoked paprika
- 1/2 teaspoon salt
- 1/4 teaspoon black pepper
- 1 tablespoon lemon juice
- 1/4 cup fresh basil, chopped

### Directions

1. Preheat the oven to 450°F. Place red bell peppers on a baking sheet and roast for 20 minutes, turning halfway, until skins are charred.
2. Remove peppers from the oven, let cool slightly, then peel off skins and remove seeds. Chop the peppers.
3. In a large pot, heat olive oil over medium heat. Add onion and garlic, sauté until onion is translucent.
4. Stir in quinoa, roasted peppers, vegetable broth, smoked paprika, salt, and black pepper. Bring to a boil, then reduce heat and simmer for 15 minutes.
5. Blend the soup until smooth using a blender. Return to the pot, stir in lemon juice and fresh basil. Adjust seasoning if needed.
6. Serve hot, garnished with additional basil if desired.

### Nutritional Information

Calories: 210, Protein: 6g, Carbohydrates: 38g, Fat: 5g, Fiber: 6g, Cholesterol: 0mg, Sodium: 600mg, Potassium: 800mg

# THAI-INSPIRED COCONUT CURRY SOUP

**Servings 4 | Prep: 15 min | Cook: 20 min**

This vibrant and aromatic Thai-inspired coconut curry soup is a delightful blend of creamy coconut milk, spicy curry paste, and fresh vegetables, offering a comforting and nutritious meal.

### Equipment

Large Pot, Wooden Spoon, Knife

### Ingredients

- 1 tbsp coconut oil
- 1 medium onion, diced
- 2 cloves garlic, minced
- 1 tbsp red curry paste
- 1 can (13.5 oz) coconut milk
- 2 cups vegetable broth
- 1 cup sliced bell peppers
- 1 cup sliced mushrooms
- 1 cup baby spinach
- 1 tbsp lime juice
- Salt and pepper to taste
- Fresh cilantro for garnish

### Directions

1. Heat coconut oil in a large pot over medium heat. Add onion and garlic, sauté until onion is translucent.
2. Stir in red curry paste and cook for 1 minute until fragrant.
3. Pour in coconut milk and vegetable broth, bring to a simmer.
4. Add bell peppers and mushrooms, cook for 5 minutes until vegetables are tender.
5. Stir in baby spinach and lime juice, season with salt and pepper. Cook for another 2 minutes.
6. Serve hot, garnished with fresh cilantro.

### Nutritional Information

Calories: 250, Protein: 4g, Carbohydrates: 18g, Fat: 20g, Fiber: 4g, Cholesterol: 0 mg, Sodium: 450 mg, Potassium: 500 mg

# MEDITERRANEAN LENTIL SOUP

**Servings 6 | Prep: 15 min | Cook: 45 min**

This hearty Mediterranean Lentil Soup is a nutritious blend of earthy lentils, vibrant vegetables, and aromatic herbs, perfect for a wholesome meal.

### Equipment

Large Pot, Wooden Spoon, Knife

### Ingredients

- 1 tbsp olive oil
- 1 medium onion, diced
- 2 cloves garlic, minced
- 1 cup carrots, diced
- 1 cup celery, diced
- 1 1/2 cups dried lentils, rinsed
- 8 cups vegetable broth
- 1 can (14.5 oz) diced tomatoes
- 1 tsp dried oregano
- 1 tsp dried thyme
- 1/2 tsp ground cumin
- Salt and pepper to taste
- 2 cups fresh spinach, chopped
- 1 tbsp lemon juice

### Directions

1. Heat olive oil in a large pot over medium heat. Add onion and garlic, sauté until translucent.
2. Stir in carrots and celery, cooking for 5 minutes until softened.
3. Add lentils, vegetable broth, diced tomatoes, oregano, thyme, cumin, salt, and pepper. Bring to a boil.
4. Reduce heat, cover, and simmer for 30-35 minutes until lentils are tender.
5. Stir in spinach and lemon juice, cooking for an additional 5 minutes. Adjust seasoning if needed.

### Nutritional Information

Calories: 210, Protein: 12g, Carbohydrates: 35g, Fat: 4g, Fiber: 12g, Cholesterol: 0mg, Sodium: 480mg, Potassium: 650mg

# GREEN PEA & MINT SOUP

**Servings 4 | Prep: 10 min | Cook: 20 min**

This refreshing Green Pea & Mint Soup is a vibrant blend of sweet peas and fresh mint, perfect for a light and healthy meal.

### Equipment

Blender, Large Pot, Wooden Spoon

### Ingredients

- 2 tbsp olive oil
- 1 medium onion, chopped
- 2 cups vegetable broth
- 16 oz frozen green peas
- 1/4 cup fresh mint leaves
- 1/2 tsp salt
- 1/4 tsp black pepper
- 1 tbsp lemon juice

### Directions

1. Heat olive oil in a large pot over medium heat. Add chopped onion and sauté until translucent, about 5 minutes.
2. Pour in the vegetable broth and bring to a boil.
3. Add the frozen green peas, reduce heat, and simmer for 5 minutes until peas are tender.
4. Stir in fresh mint leaves, salt, and black pepper.
5. Remove from heat and blend the mixture until smooth using a blender.
6. Stir in lemon juice and adjust seasoning if necessary.
7. Serve warm, garnished with additional mint leaves if desired.

### Nutritional Information

Calories: 180, Protein: 6g, Carbohydrates: 24g, Fat: 8g, Fiber: 6g, Cholesterol: 0mg, Sodium: 450mg, Potassium: 350mg

## DETOX CABBAGE SOUP

**Servings 6 | Prep: 15 min | Cook: 30 min**

This nourishing Detox Cabbage Soup is a perfect blend of fresh vegetables and herbs, designed to cleanse and rejuvenate your body while delighting your taste buds.

### Equipment

Large Pot, Cutting Board, Knife

### Ingredients

- 1 tbsp olive oil
- 1 medium onion, chopped
- 2 cloves garlic, minced
- 1 medium head of cabbage, chopped
- 2 carrots, sliced
- 2 stalks celery, sliced
- 1 bell pepper, chopped
- 6 cups vegetable broth
- 1 can (14.5 oz) diced tomatoes
- 1 tsp dried oregano
- 1 tsp dried basil
- Salt and pepper to taste
- 1 tbsp lemon juice
- 1/4 cup fresh parsley, chopped

### Directions

1. Heat olive oil in a large pot over medium heat. Add onion and garlic, sauté until fragrant.
2. Stir in cabbage, carrots, celery, and bell pepper. Cook for 5 minutes, stirring occasionally.
3. Pour in vegetable broth and diced tomatoes. Add oregano, basil, salt, and pepper.
4. Bring to a boil, then reduce heat and simmer for 20 minutes, until vegetables are tender.
5. Stir in lemon juice and fresh parsley before serving.

### Nutritional Information

Calories: 90, Protein: 3g, Carbohydrates: 18g, Fat: 2g, Fiber: 5g, Cholesterol: 0mg, Sodium: 480mg, Potassium: 450mg

## BLACK BEAN & SWEET POTATO STEW

**Servings 4 | Prep: 15 min | Cook: 30 min**

This hearty and nutritious stew combines the earthy flavors of black beans with the natural sweetness of sweet potatoes, creating a comforting dish perfect for any season.

### Equipment

Large Pot, Wooden Spoon, Knife

### Ingredients

- 1 tbsp olive oil
- 1 medium onion, diced
- 2 cloves garlic, minced
- 1 lb sweet potatoes, peeled and cubed
- 2 cups vegetable broth
- 1 can (15 oz) black beans, drained and rinsed
- 1 can (14.5 oz) diced tomatoes
- 1 tsp ground cumin
- 1 tsp chili powder
- Salt and pepper to taste
- 1/4 cup fresh cilantro, chopped (optional)

### Directions

1. Heat olive oil in a large pot over medium heat. Add onion and garlic; sauté until onion is translucent.
2. Stir in sweet potatoes, vegetable broth, black beans, and diced tomatoes.
3. Add cumin, chili powder, salt, and pepper. Bring to a boil, then reduce heat and simmer for 20-25 minutes until sweet potatoes are tender.
4. Adjust seasoning if necessary.
5. Serve hot, garnished with fresh cilantro if desired.

### Nutritional Information

Calories: 250, Protein: 8g, Carbohydrates: 45g, Fat: 5g, Fiber: 12g, Cholesterol: 0mg, Sodium: 600mg, Potassium: 800mg

# GINGER & TURMERIC IMMUNE BOOST SOUP

**Servings 4 | Prep: 10 min | Cook: 25 min**

This vibrant and nourishing soup combines the anti-inflammatory properties of ginger and turmeric to create a comforting bowl that supports your immune system. Perfect for chilly days or when you need a health boost.

### Equipment

Large Pot, Cutting Board, Knife

### Ingredients

- 1 tbsp olive oil
- 1 medium onion, chopped
- 2 cloves garlic, minced
- 1 tbsp fresh ginger, grated
- 1 tsp ground turmeric
- 4 cups vegetable broth
- 1 cup carrots, sliced
- 1 cup sweet potatoes, diced
- 1 cup kale, chopped
- 1 tbsp lemon juice
- Salt and pepper to taste

### Directions

1. Heat olive oil in a large pot over medium heat. Add onion and sauté until translucent.
2. Stir in garlic, ginger, and turmeric, cooking for 1 minute until fragrant.
3. Add vegetable broth, carrots, and sweet potatoes. Bring to a boil, then reduce heat and simmer for 15 minutes.
4. Stir in kale and cook for an additional 5 minutes until wilted.
5. Add lemon juice, and season with salt and pepper to taste. Serve warm.

### Nutritional Information

Calories: 150, Protein: 3g, Carbohydrates: 25g, Fat: 5g, Fiber: 5g, Cholesterol: 0mg, Sodium: 600mg, Potassium: 450mg

# PUMPKIN & WHITE BEAN SOUP

**Servings 4 | Prep: 10 min | Cook: 30 min**

A comforting and hearty soup that combines the creamy texture of pumpkin with the protein-rich goodness of white beans, perfect for a cozy meal.

### Equipment

Large Pot, Blender or Immersion Blender, Ladle

### Ingredients

- 2 tbsp olive oil
- 1 medium onion, chopped
- 2 cloves garlic, minced
- 15 oz canned pumpkin puree
- 4 cups vegetable broth
- 15 oz canned white beans, drained and rinsed
- 1 tsp ground cumin
- 1/2 tsp ground cinnamon
- Salt and pepper to taste
- 1/4 cup fresh parsley, chopped (optional for garnish)

### Directions

1. Heat olive oil in a large pot over medium heat. Add onion and garlic, sauté until onion is translucent.
2. Stir in pumpkin puree, vegetable broth, white beans, cumin, and cinnamon. Bring to a boil.
3. Reduce heat and let simmer for 20 minutes, stirring occasionally.
4. Use a blender or immersion blender to puree the soup until smooth.
5. Season with salt and pepper to taste.
6. Serve hot, garnished with fresh parsley if desired.

### Nutritional Information

Calories: 210, Protein: 8g, Carbohydrates: 32g, Fat: 7g, Fiber: 9g, Cholesterol: 0mg, Sodium: 480mg, Potassium: 600mg

# CHICKPEA & SPINACH STEW

**Servings 4 | Prep: 10 min | Cook: 30 min**

This hearty Chickpea & Spinach Stew is a nourishing blend of flavors, perfect for a cozy meal. Packed with protein and fiber, it's a clean eating delight that warms the soul.

### Equipment

Large Pot, Wooden Spoon, Measuring Cups and Spoons

### Ingredients

- 2 tbsp olive oil
- 1 medium onion, chopped
- 2 cloves garlic, minced
- 1 tsp ground cumin
- 1/2 tsp smoked paprika
- 1 can (15 oz) chickpeas, drained and rinsed
- 4 cups vegetable broth
- 4 cups fresh spinach
- 1 can (14.5 oz) diced tomatoes
- Salt and pepper to taste

### Directions

1. Heat olive oil in a large pot over medium heat. Add onion and garlic; sauté until onion is translucent.
2. Stir in cumin and smoked paprika; cook for 1 minute until fragrant.
3. Add chickpeas, vegetable broth, and diced tomatoes. Bring to a boil, then reduce heat and simmer for 20 minutes.
4. Stir in fresh spinach and cook until wilted, about 2-3 minutes.
5. Season with salt and pepper to taste. Serve hot.

### Nutritional Information

Calories: 220, Protein: 8g, Carbohydrates: 32g, Fat: 8g, Fiber: 8g, Cholesterol: 0mg, Sodium: 600mg, Potassium: 750mg

# SAVORY ROASTED GARLIC SOUP

**Servings 4 | Prep: 10 min | Cook: 40 min**

This creamy, aromatic soup is a celebration of roasted garlic, offering a rich and comforting flavor perfect for any season.

### Equipment

Baking Sheet, Blender, Saucepan

### Ingredients

- 2 heads garlic
- 2 tbsp olive oil
- 1 medium onion, chopped
- 4 cups vegetable broth
- 1 cup unsweetened almond milk
- 1 tsp thyme
- Salt and pepper to taste

### Directions

1. Preheat oven to 400°F. Slice the tops off garlic heads, drizzle with 1 tbsp olive oil, wrap in foil, and roast for 30 minutes until soft.
2. In a saucepan, heat 1 tbsp olive oil over medium heat. Sauté onion until translucent.
3. Squeeze roasted garlic cloves into the saucepan. Add vegetable broth and thyme. Simmer for 10 minutes.
4. Blend the mixture until smooth. Return to saucepan, stir in almond milk, and heat through.
5. Season with salt and pepper to taste. Serve warm.

### Nutritional Information

Calories: 150, Protein: 3g, Carbohydrates: 18g, Fat: 8g, Fiber: 2g, Cholesterol: 0mg, Sodium: 400mg, Potassium: 350mg

# ZUCCHINI & BASIL CREAM SOUP

**Servings 4 | Prep: 10 min | Cook: 20 min**

This Zucchini & Basil Cream Soup is a refreshing and creamy delight, perfect for a light lunch or a starter. The fresh basil adds a fragrant touch, making it a comforting yet invigorating dish.

### Equipment

Large Pot, Blender, Ladle

### Ingredients

- 1 tbsp olive oil
- 1 medium onion, chopped
- 2 cloves garlic, minced
- 1 lb zucchini, sliced
- 4 cups vegetable broth
- 1 cup fresh basil leaves
- 1/2 cup unsweetened almond milk
- Salt and pepper to taste

### Directions

1. Heat olive oil in a large pot over medium heat. Add the onion and garlic, sauté until the onion is translucent.
2. Add the zucchini slices and cook for about 5 minutes, stirring occasionally.
3. Pour in the vegetable broth, bring to a boil, then reduce heat and simmer for 15 minutes until zucchini is tender.
4. Transfer the mixture to a blender, add basil leaves, and blend until smooth.
5. Return the soup to the pot, stir in almond milk, and season with salt and pepper. Heat gently before serving.

### Nutritional Information

Calories: 120, Protein: 3g, Carbohydrates: 15g, Fat: 7g, Fiber: 3g, Cholesterol: 0mg, Sodium: 500mg, Potassium: 600mg

# MUSHROOM & WILD RICE SOUP

**Servings 4 | Prep: 15 min | Cook: 45 min**

This hearty and earthy Mushroom & Wild Rice Soup is a perfect blend of flavors and textures, offering a comforting and nutritious meal that embodies the essence of clean eating.

### Equipment

Large Pot, Cutting Board, Knife

### Ingredients

- 1 tbsp olive oil
- 1 cup wild rice
- 8 oz cremini mushrooms, sliced
- 1 medium onion, diced
- 2 cloves garlic, minced
- 4 cups vegetable broth
- 1 cup water
- 1 tsp dried thyme
- 1/2 tsp salt
- 1/4 tsp black pepper
- 1 cup kale, chopped

### Directions

1. Heat olive oil in a large pot over medium heat. Add onions and garlic, sauté until translucent.
2. Stir in mushrooms and cook until they release their moisture and begin to brown.
3. Add wild rice, vegetable broth, water, thyme, salt, and pepper. Bring to a boil.
4. Reduce heat to low, cover, and simmer for 40 minutes, or until rice is tender.
5. Stir in kale and cook for an additional 5 minutes until wilted.
6. Adjust seasoning to taste and serve hot.

### Nutritional Information

Calories: 210, Protein: 6g, Carbohydrates: 35g, Fat: 5g, Fiber: 4g, Cholesterol: 0mg, Sodium: 550mg, Potassium: 450mg

# TOMATO & ROASTED RED PEPPER STEW

**Servings 4 | Prep: 15 min | Cook: 30 min**

This hearty stew combines the rich flavors of tomatoes and roasted red peppers, creating a comforting and nutritious dish perfect for any season.

### Equipment

Large Pot, Blender, Wooden Spoon

### Ingredients

- 2 tbsp olive oil
- 1 medium onion, chopped
- 2 cloves garlic, minced
- 1 lb tomatoes, chopped
- 12 oz jar roasted red peppers, drained and chopped
- 2 cups vegetable broth
- 1 tsp dried basil
- 1/2 tsp salt
- 1/4 tsp black pepper

### Directions

1. Heat olive oil in a large pot over medium heat. Add onion and garlic, sauté until soft.
2. Stir in tomatoes and roasted red peppers, cooking for 5 minutes.
3. Add vegetable broth, basil, salt, and black pepper. Bring to a boil, then reduce heat and simmer for 20 minutes.
4. Use a blender to puree the stew until smooth. Return to pot and heat through.
5. Adjust seasoning if necessary and serve hot.

### Nutritional Information

Calories: 180, Protein: 3g, Carbohydrates: 20g, Fat: 10g, Fiber: 4g, Cholesterol: 0mg, Sodium: 600mg, Potassium: 700mg

# KALE & WHITE BEAN SOUP

**Servings 4 | Prep: 10 min | Cook: 30 min**

This hearty and nourishing soup combines the earthy flavors of kale with the creamy texture of white beans, creating a comforting dish perfect for any season.

### Equipment

Large Pot, Wooden Spoon, Ladle

### Ingredients

- 1 tbsp olive oil
- 1 medium onion, chopped
- 2 cloves garlic, minced
- 4 cups vegetable broth
- 1 can (15 oz) white beans, drained and rinsed
- 4 cups kale, chopped
- 1 tsp dried thyme
- 1/2 tsp salt
- 1/4 tsp black pepper

### Directions

1. Heat olive oil in a large pot over medium heat. Add onion and garlic, sauté until onion is translucent.
2. Pour in vegetable broth and bring to a simmer.
3. Stir in white beans, kale, thyme, salt, and pepper.
4. Cover and cook for 20 minutes, until kale is tender.
5. Adjust seasoning to taste and serve hot.

### Nutritional Information

Calories: 180, Protein: 8g, Carbohydrates: 28g, Fat: 5g, Fiber: 7g, Cholesterol: 0 mg, Sodium: 580 mg, Potassium: 600 mg

## SPICY CAULIFLOWER SOUP

**Servings 4 | Prep: 10 min | Cook: 25 min**

This Spicy Cauliflower Soup is a warming, flavorful dish that combines the earthy taste of cauliflower with a kick of spice, perfect for a cozy meal.

### Equipment

Large Pot, Blender, Ladle

### Ingredients

- 1 tbsp olive oil
- 1 medium onion, chopped
- 2 cloves garlic, minced
- 1 medium cauliflower, chopped (about 1.5 lbs)
- 4 cups vegetable broth
- 1 tsp ground cumin
- 1/2 tsp cayenne pepper
- Salt and pepper to taste
- 1/4 cup fresh cilantro, chopped (for garnish)

### Directions

1. Heat olive oil in a large pot over medium heat. Add onion and garlic, sauté until onion is translucent.
2. Add chopped cauliflower, vegetable broth, cumin, and cayenne pepper. Bring to a boil, then reduce heat and simmer for 20 minutes, until cauliflower is tender.
3. Carefully transfer the soup to a blender and blend until smooth. Return to the pot and season with salt and pepper.
4. Serve hot, garnished with fresh cilantro.

### Nutritional Information

Calories: 120, Protein: 4g, Carbohydrates: 18g, Fat: 5g, Fiber: 5g, Cholesterol: 0mg, Sodium: 600mg, Potassium: 450mg

## LEMON & PARSNIP SOUP

**Servings 4 | Prep: 15 min | Cook: 30 min**

This refreshing and creamy Lemon & Parsnip Soup combines the earthy sweetness of parsnips with the bright zest of lemon, creating a comforting yet invigorating dish perfect for any season.

### Equipment

Large Pot, Blender, Knife

### Ingredients

- 1 lb parsnips, peeled and chopped
- 1 tbsp olive oil
- 1 medium onion, chopped
- 2 cloves garlic, minced
- 4 cups vegetable broth
- 1 lemon, zest and juice
- 1 tsp salt
- 1/2 tsp black pepper
- 1/4 cup fresh parsley, chopped

### Directions

1. Heat olive oil in a large pot over medium heat. Add onion and garlic, sauté until onion is translucent.
2. Add chopped parsnips to the pot, stirring occasionally for about 5 minutes.
3. Pour in the vegetable broth, bring to a boil, then reduce heat and simmer until parsnips are tender, about 20 minutes.
4. Remove from heat and blend the soup until smooth using a blender.
5. Stir in lemon zest, juice, salt, and pepper. Adjust seasoning to taste.
6. Serve hot, garnished with fresh parsley.

### Nutritional Information

Calories: 150, Protein: 3g, Carbohydrates: 30g, Fat: 4g, Fiber: 7g, Cholesterol: 0 mg, Sodium: 600 mg, Potassium: 500 mg

# Main Dishes

## GRILLED LEMON HERB CHICKEN

**Servings 4 | Prep: 15 min | Cook: 20 min**

This Grilled Lemon Herb Chicken is a refreshing and flavorful dish, perfect for a clean eating lifestyle. The zesty lemon and aromatic herbs infuse the chicken with a delightful taste, making it a healthy and satisfying main course.

### Equipment

Grill, Mixing Bowl, Tongs

### Ingredients

- 1.5 lbs boneless, skinless chicken breasts
- 1/4 cup fresh lemon juice
- 2 tbsp olive oil
- 2 tsp dried oregano
- 2 tsp dried thyme
- 1 tsp garlic powder
- 1/2 tsp salt
- 1/4 tsp black pepper
- 1 lemon, sliced for garnish

### Directions

1. In a mixing bowl, combine lemon juice, olive oil, oregano, thyme, garlic powder, salt, and black pepper.
2. Place chicken breasts in the bowl and coat them evenly with the marinade. Let it marinate for at least 15 minutes.
3. Preheat the grill to medium-high heat.
4. Grill the chicken for 6-7 minutes on each side, or until the internal temperature reaches 165°F.
5. Remove from the grill and let it rest for a few minutes. Garnish with lemon slices before serving.

### Nutritional Information

Calories: 250, Protein: 38g, Carbohydrates: 2g, Fat: 10g, Fiber: 0g, Cholesterol: 95mg, Sodium: 320mg, Potassium: 450mg

## BAKED SALMON WITH GARLIC & DILL

**Servings 4 | Prep: 10 min | Cook: 20 min**

This dish features tender, flaky salmon infused with the fresh flavors of garlic and dill, offering a nutritious and satisfying main course that's perfect for clean eating enthusiasts.

### Equipment

Baking Sheet, Mixing Bowl, Aluminum Foil

### Ingredients

- 1 lb salmon fillet
- 2 tbsp olive oil
- 3 cloves garlic, minced
- 2 tbsp fresh dill, chopped
- 1 lemon, sliced
- 1 tsp sea salt
- 1/2 tsp black pepper

### Directions

1. Preheat the oven to 400°F (200°C).
2. Line a baking sheet with aluminum foil and place the salmon fillet on it.
3. In a mixing bowl, combine olive oil, minced garlic, chopped dill, sea salt, and black pepper.
4. Spread the garlic and dill mixture evenly over the salmon fillet.
5. Arrange lemon slices on top of the salmon.
6. Fold the foil over the salmon to create a sealed packet.
7. Bake in the preheated oven for 20 minutes, or until the salmon is cooked through and flakes easily with a fork.

### Nutritional Information

Calories: 280, Protein: 25g, Carbohydrates: 2g, Fat: 19g, Fiber: 0g, Cholesterol: 60mg, Sodium: 320mg, Potassium: 650mg

# STUFFED BELL PEPPERS WITH QUINOA & BLACK BEANS

**Servings 4 | Prep: 15 min | Cook: 30 min**

These vibrant stuffed bell peppers are filled with a hearty mix of quinoa and black beans, offering a nutritious and satisfying main dish that's perfect for clean eating.

### Equipment

Large Pot, Baking Dish, Mixing Bowl

### Ingredients

- 4 large bell peppers, tops removed and seeds cleaned
- 1 cup quinoa, rinsed
- 2 cups vegetable broth
- 1 can (15 oz) black beans, drained and rinsed
- 1 cup corn kernels (fresh or frozen)
- 1 cup diced tomatoes
- 1 tsp cumin
- 1 tsp chili powder
- 1/2 tsp salt
- 1/4 tsp black pepper
- 1/4 cup chopped fresh cilantro

### Directions

1. Preheat the oven to 375°F (190°C).
2. In a large pot, bring the vegetable broth to a boil. Add quinoa, reduce heat to low, cover, and simmer for 15 minutes or until the liquid is absorbed.
3. In a mixing bowl, combine cooked quinoa, black beans, corn, diced tomatoes, cumin, chili powder, salt, and black pepper. Mix well.
4. Stuff each bell pepper with the quinoa mixture and place them upright in a baking dish.
5. Cover the dish with foil and bake for 25-30 minutes, until the peppers are tender.
6. Remove from the oven, garnish with fresh cilantro, and serve warm.

### Nutritional Information

Calories: 250, Protein: 10g, Carbohydrates: 45g, Fat: 4g, Fiber: 10g, Cholesterol: 0mg, Sodium: 400mg, Potassium: 800mg

# CHICKPEA & SWEET POTATO BUDDHA BOWL

**Servings 4 | Prep: 15 min | Cook: 30 min**

This vibrant Buddha bowl combines roasted sweet potatoes and chickpeas with fresh greens and a tangy tahini dressing, offering a nourishing and satisfying meal.

### Equipment

Baking Sheet, Mixing Bowl, Whisk

### Ingredients

- 2 medium sweet potatoes, peeled and cubed
- 1 can (15 oz) chickpeas, drained and rinsed
- 2 tbsp olive oil
- 1 tsp ground cumin
- 1 tsp paprika
- 1/2 tsp salt
- 4 cups mixed greens
- 1 avocado, sliced
- 1/4 cup tahini
- 2 tbsp lemon juice
- 2 tbsp water
- 1 clove garlic, minced

### Directions

1. Preheat the oven to 400°F (200°C).
2. Toss sweet potatoes and chickpeas with olive oil, cumin, paprika, and salt on a baking sheet.
3. Roast for 25-30 minutes, stirring halfway, until sweet potatoes are tender.
4. In a mixing bowl, whisk together tahini, lemon juice, water, and garlic to make the dressing.
5. Divide mixed greens among four bowls, top with roasted sweet potatoes, chickpeas, and avocado slices.
6. Drizzle with tahini dressing before serving.

### Nutritional Information

Calories: 350, Protein: 9g, Carbohydrates: 45g, Fat: 18g, Fiber: 12g, Cholesterol: 0mg, Sodium: 350mg, Potassium: 950mg

## ZUCCHINI NOODLES WITH PESTO

**Servings 4 | Prep: 15 min | Cook: 5 min**

A refreshing and light dish, Zucchini Noodles with Pesto offers a delightful twist on traditional pasta, combining the fresh taste of zucchini with the rich flavors of homemade pesto.

### Equipment

Spiralizer, Blender, Large Skillet

### Ingredients

- 4 medium zucchinis (about 1.5 lbs)
- 2 cups fresh basil leaves
- 1/2 cup pine nuts
- 1/2 cup grated Parmesan cheese
- 2 cloves garlic
- 1/2 cup extra-virgin olive oil
- 1/4 tsp salt
- 1/4 tsp black pepper
- 1 tbsp lemon juice

### Directions

1. Spiralize the zucchinis into noodles using a spiralizer.
2. In a blender, combine basil leaves, pine nuts, Parmesan cheese, garlic, olive oil, salt, and pepper. Blend until smooth to make the pesto.
3. Heat a large skillet over medium heat. Add the zucchini noodles and sauté for 2-3 minutes until just tender.
4. Remove the skillet from heat and toss the zucchini noodles with the pesto and lemon juice until well coated.
5. Serve immediately, garnished with additional Parmesan cheese if desired.

### Nutritional Information

Calories: 320, Protein: 8g, Carbohydrates: 10g, Fat: 30g, Fiber: 3g, Cholesterol: 10mg, Sodium: 200mg, Potassium: 550mg

## LENTIL & VEGETABLE STIR-FRY

**Servings 4 | Prep: 15 min | Cook: 20 min**

A vibrant and nutritious dish, this Lentil & Vegetable Stir-Fry combines the earthy flavors of lentils with the crispness of fresh vegetables, all brought together with a light, savory sauce. Perfect for a quick and healthy dinner.

### Equipment

Large Skillet, Medium Saucepan, Wooden Spoon

### Ingredients

- 1 cup green lentils
- 2 cups water
- 2 tbsp olive oil
- 1 medium red bell pepper, sliced
- 1 medium carrot, julienned
- 1 cup broccoli florets
- 1 small onion, thinly sliced
- 2 cloves garlic, minced
- 2 tbsp soy sauce
- 1 tbsp sesame seeds
- 1 tsp fresh ginger, grated
- 1/4 cup green onions, chopped

### Directions

1. Rinse lentils under cold water. In a medium saucepan, combine lentils and water. Bring to a boil, then reduce heat and simmer for 15-20 minutes until tender. Drain and set aside.
2. In a large skillet, heat olive oil over medium heat. Add onion and garlic, sauté until fragrant.
3. Add bell pepper, carrot, and broccoli to the skillet. Stir-fry for 5-7 minutes until vegetables are tender-crisp.
4. Stir in cooked lentils, soy sauce, and ginger. Cook for an additional 2-3 minutes, stirring frequently.
5. Sprinkle with sesame seeds and green onions before serving.

### Nutritional Information

Calories: 250, Protein: 12g, Carbohydrates: 38g, Fat: 7g, Fiber: 12g, Cholesterol: 0mg, Sodium: 420mg, Potassium: 600mg

# GARLIC & HERB ROASTED TOFU

**Servings 4 | Prep: 15 min | Cook: 30 min**

This dish features tofu infused with a savory blend of garlic and herbs, roasted to perfection for a satisfying, protein-rich main course.

### Equipment

Baking Sheet, Mixing Bowl, Whisk

### Ingredients

- 14 oz extra-firm tofu, drained and pressed
- 2 tbsp olive oil
- 3 cloves garlic, minced
- 1 tbsp fresh rosemary, chopped
- 1 tbsp fresh thyme, chopped
- 1 tsp salt
- 1/2 tsp black pepper
- 1 lemon, juiced

### Directions

1. Preheat the oven to 400°F (200°C).
2. Cut the tofu into 1-inch cubes and place them in a mixing bowl.
3. In a separate bowl, whisk together olive oil, garlic, rosemary, thyme, salt, pepper, and lemon juice.
4. Pour the marinade over the tofu, tossing gently to coat evenly.
5. Arrange the tofu cubes on a baking sheet in a single layer.
6. Roast in the preheated oven for 25-30 minutes, flipping halfway through, until golden and crisp.

### Nutritional Information

Calories: 180, Protein: 10g, Carbohydrates: 6g, Fat: 14g, Fiber: 2g, Cholesterol: 0mg, Sodium: 590mg, Potassium: 200mg

# MEDITERRANEAN STUFFED EGGPLANT

**Servings 4 | Prep: 15 min | Cook: 40 min**

This Mediterranean Stuffed Eggplant is a delightful blend of fresh vegetables, herbs, and spices, creating a wholesome and flavorful main dish that embodies the essence of clean eating.

### Equipment

Baking Sheet, Large Skillet, Mixing Bowl

### Ingredients

- 2 medium eggplants, halved lengthwise
- 2 tbsp olive oil
- 1 cup cherry tomatoes, halved
- 1 cup cooked quinoa
- 1/2 cup crumbled feta cheese
- 1/4 cup chopped fresh parsley
- 1/4 cup chopped red onion
- 2 cloves garlic, minced
- 1 tsp dried oregano
- Salt and pepper to taste

### Directions

1. Preheat the oven to 375°F (190°C). Scoop out the flesh of the eggplants, leaving a 1/2-inch shell, and chop the flesh.
2. Brush the eggplant shells with 1 tbsp olive oil, place them on a baking sheet, and bake for 20 minutes.
3. In a large skillet, heat the remaining olive oil over medium heat. Sauté the chopped eggplant flesh, cherry tomatoes, red onion, and garlic until softened, about 5-7 minutes.
4. In a mixing bowl, combine the sautéed vegetables with quinoa, feta cheese, parsley, oregano, salt, and pepper.
5. Stuff the eggplant shells with the mixture, return to the oven, and bake for an additional 15-20 minutes until heated through and slightly golden on top.

### Nutritional Information

Calories: 210, Protein: 7g, Carbohydrates: 25g, Fat: 10g, Fiber: 7g, Cholesterol: 10mg, Sodium: 220mg, Potassium: 680mg

# BALSAMIC GLAZED CHICKEN BREAST

**Servings 4 | Prep: 10 min | Cook: 20 min**

This dish features tender chicken breasts coated in a rich, tangy balsamic glaze, perfect for a healthy and flavorful main course.

### Equipment

Skillet, Mixing Bowl, Whisk

### Ingredients

- 1 lb boneless, skinless chicken breasts
- 1/2 cup balsamic vinegar
- 2 tbsp honey
- 1 tbsp olive oil
- 2 cloves garlic, minced
- 1/2 tsp salt
- 1/4 tsp black pepper

### Directions

1. Season the chicken breasts with salt and pepper on both sides.
2. In a mixing bowl, whisk together balsamic vinegar, honey, and minced garlic.
3. Heat olive oil in a skillet over medium heat. Add chicken breasts and cook for 5-6 minutes on each side, until golden brown.
4. Pour the balsamic mixture over the chicken in the skillet. Reduce heat to low and simmer for 10 minutes, turning the chicken occasionally, until the glaze thickens.
5. Serve the chicken breasts drizzled with the balsamic glaze.

### Nutritional Information

Calories: 210, Protein: 28g, Carbohydrates: 12g, Fat: 6g, Fiber: 0g, Cholesterol: 70mg, Sodium: 320mg, Potassium: 450mg

# SPAGHETTI SQUASH & TOMATO SAUCE

**Servings 4 | Prep: 15 min | Cook: 45 min**

This dish transforms spaghetti squash into a delightful, low-carb alternative to traditional pasta, paired with a rich and savory tomato sauce that bursts with flavor.

### Equipment

Oven, Baking Sheet, Large Skillet

### Ingredients

- 1 medium spaghetti squash (about 3 lbs)
- 2 tbsp olive oil
- 1 small onion, diced
- 2 cloves garlic, minced
- 1 can (14.5 oz) crushed tomatoes
- 1 tsp dried oregano
- 1/2 tsp salt
- 1/4 tsp black pepper
- 1/4 cup fresh basil, chopped

### Directions

1. Preheat the oven to 400°F (200°C). Cut the spaghetti squash in half lengthwise and remove the seeds.
2. Place the squash halves cut-side down on a baking sheet. Roast for 35-40 minutes until tender.
3. While the squash is roasting, heat olive oil in a large skillet over medium heat. Add onion and garlic, sauté until translucent.
4. Stir in crushed tomatoes, oregano, salt, and pepper. Simmer for 10 minutes, stirring occasionally.
5. Once the squash is cooked, use a fork to scrape out the strands. Serve topped with tomato sauce and fresh basil.

### Nutritional Information

Calories: 180, Protein: 4g, Carbohydrates: 28g, Fat: 8g, Fiber: 6g, Cholesterol: 0mg, Sodium: 320mg, Potassium: 780mg

# TURMERIC ROASTED CAULIFLOWER STEAKS

**Servings 4 | Prep: 10 min | Cook: 30 min**

These vibrant turmeric roasted cauliflower steaks are a delicious and nutritious main dish, offering a perfect blend of spices and a satisfying crunch.

### Equipment

Baking Sheet, Mixing Bowl, Chef's Knife

### Ingredients

- 1 large head of cauliflower (about 2 lbs)
- 3 tbsp olive oil
- 1 tsp ground turmeric
- 1 tsp ground cumin
- 1/2 tsp garlic powder
- 1/2 tsp salt
- 1/4 tsp black pepper
- 1 tbsp lemon juice
- 2 tbsp chopped fresh parsley (optional, for garnish)

### Directions

1. Preheat the oven to 400°F (200°C).
2. Remove the leaves and trim the stem of the cauliflower, then slice it into 1-inch thick steaks.
3. In a mixing bowl, combine olive oil, turmeric, cumin, garlic powder, salt, and black pepper.
4. Brush the cauliflower steaks with the spice mixture on both sides.
5. Place the steaks on a baking sheet and roast for 25-30 minutes, flipping halfway through, until golden and tender.
6. Drizzle with lemon juice and garnish with fresh parsley before serving.

### Nutritional Information

Calories: 120, Protein: 3g, Carbohydrates: 10g, Fat: 9g, Fiber: 4g, Cholesterol: 0mg, Sodium: 310mg, Potassium: 450mg

# AVOCADO & BLACK BEAN WRAPS

**Servings 4 | Prep: 15 min | Cook: 0 min**

These Avocado & Black Bean Wraps are a fresh and satisfying main dish, perfect for a quick lunch or light dinner. Packed with creamy avocado, protein-rich black beans, and crisp vegetables, these wraps are both nutritious and delicious.

### Equipment

Cutting Board, Knife, Mixing Bowl

### Ingredients

- 2 ripe avocados, peeled and pitted
- 1 cup canned black beans, drained and rinsed
- 1 cup cherry tomatoes, halved
- 1/2 cup red onion, finely chopped
- 1/4 cup fresh cilantro, chopped
- 1 tablespoon lime juice
- 1/2 teaspoon ground cumin
- 1/4 teaspoon salt
- 4 whole wheat tortillas

### Directions

1. In a mixing bowl, mash the avocados with a fork until smooth.
2. Add black beans, cherry tomatoes, red onion, cilantro, lime juice, cumin, and salt to the mashed avocados. Stir until well combined.
3. Lay out the tortillas on a flat surface. Divide the avocado and black bean mixture evenly among the tortillas.
4. Roll each tortilla tightly, tucking in the sides as you go, to form a wrap.
5. Slice each wrap in half and serve immediately.

### Nutritional Information

Calories: 320, Protein: 8g, Carbohydrates: 45g, Fat: 14g, Fiber: 12g, Cholesterol: 0mg, Sodium: 320mg, Potassium: 780mg

# HONEY MUSTARD BAKED TEMPEH

**Servings 4 | Prep: 10 min | Cook: 25 min**

This Honey Mustard Baked Tempeh is a delightful blend of sweet and tangy flavors, perfect for a wholesome and satisfying main dish.

### Equipment

Baking Dish, Mixing Bowl, Whisk

### Ingredients

- 8 oz tempeh, sliced into thin strips
- 1/4 cup honey
- 3 tbsp Dijon mustard
- 2 tbsp apple cider vinegar
- 1 tbsp olive oil
- 1/2 tsp garlic powder
- Salt and pepper to taste

### Directions

1. Preheat the oven to 375°F (190°C).
2. In a mixing bowl, whisk together honey, Dijon mustard, apple cider vinegar, olive oil, garlic powder, salt, and pepper until well combined.
3. Arrange the tempeh slices in a baking dish and pour the honey mustard mixture over them, ensuring each piece is well coated.
4. Bake in the preheated oven for 25 minutes, flipping the tempeh halfway through to ensure even cooking.
5. Remove from the oven and let it cool slightly before serving.

### Nutritional Information

Calories: 210, Protein: 12g, Carbohydrates: 22g, Fat: 9g, Fiber: 3g, Cholesterol: 0mg, Sodium: 250mg, Potassium: 250mg

# QUINOA & KALE POWER BOWL

**Servings 4 | Prep: 15 min | Cook: 20 min**

This vibrant Quinoa & Kale Power Bowl is a nutrient-packed dish that combines the earthy flavors of quinoa and kale with the freshness of cherry tomatoes and the creaminess of avocado. Perfect for a wholesome lunch or dinner, it's both satisfying and energizing.

### Equipment

Medium Saucepan, Large Mixing Bowl, Skillet

### Ingredients

- 1 cup quinoa
- 2 cups water
- 1 tbsp olive oil
- 4 cups kale, chopped
- 1 cup cherry tomatoes, halved
- 1 avocado, diced
- 1/4 cup red onion, finely chopped
- 1/4 cup feta cheese, crumbled
- 2 tbsp lemon juice
- Salt and pepper to taste

### Directions

1. Rinse the quinoa under cold water. In a medium saucepan, combine quinoa and water. Bring to a boil, then reduce heat to low, cover, and simmer for 15 minutes or until water is absorbed.
2. In a large mixing bowl, massage the chopped kale with olive oil until it becomes tender.
3. In a skillet over medium heat, lightly sauté the cherry tomatoes and red onion for 3-4 minutes until softened.
4. Combine the cooked quinoa, kale, sautéed tomatoes, and onion in the mixing bowl. Add diced avocado and crumbled feta cheese.
5. Drizzle with lemon juice, and season with salt and pepper. Toss gently to combine all ingredients.
6. Serve immediately or chill for 30 minutes for a refreshing cold salad.

### Nutritional Information

Calories: 320, Protein: 9g, Carbohydrates: 40g, Fat: 15g, Fiber: 8g, Cholesterol: 10mg, Sodium: 220mg, Potassium: 700mg

# THAI-INSPIRED TOFU CURRY

**Servings 4 | Prep: 15 min | Cook: 20 min**

This vibrant Thai-inspired tofu curry is a delightful blend of creamy coconut milk, aromatic spices, and fresh vegetables, offering a wholesome and satisfying main dish.

### Equipment

Large Skillet, Cutting Board, Knife

### Ingredients

- 14 oz firm tofu, drained and cubed
- 1 tbsp coconut oil
- 1 cup coconut milk
- 2 tbsp red curry paste
- 1 red bell pepper, sliced
- 1 cup broccoli florets
- 1 tbsp soy sauce
- 1 tsp grated ginger
- 2 cloves garlic, minced
- 1 tbsp lime juice
- 1/4 cup fresh basil leaves

### Directions

1. Heat coconut oil in a large skillet over medium heat. Add tofu cubes and cook until golden brown on all sides. Remove and set aside.
2. In the same skillet, add garlic and ginger, sautéing until fragrant.
3. Stir in red curry paste and coconut milk, mixing until well combined.
4. Add bell pepper and broccoli, cooking until vegetables are tender-crisp.
5. Return tofu to the skillet, adding soy sauce and lime juice. Stir to coat everything evenly.
6. Simmer for a few minutes, allowing flavors to meld.
7. Garnish with fresh basil leaves before serving.

### Nutritional Information

Calories: 280, Protein: 12g, Carbohydrates: 14g, Fat: 20g, Fiber: 4g, Cholesterol: 0mg, Sodium: 420mg, Potassium: 450mg

# SPINACH & CHICKPEA STIR-FRY

**Servings 4 | Prep: 10 min | Cook: 15 min**

A vibrant and nutritious stir-fry that combines the earthy flavors of spinach with the hearty texture of chickpeas, perfect for a wholesome meal.

### Equipment

Large Skillet, Wooden Spoon, Measuring Cups and Spoons

### Ingredients

- 1 tablespoon olive oil
- 1 medium onion, sliced
- 2 cloves garlic, minced
- 1 (15 oz) can chickpeas, drained and rinsed
- 8 oz fresh spinach leaves
- 1 teaspoon ground cumin
- 1/2 teaspoon paprika
- Salt and pepper to taste
- 1 tablespoon lemon juice

### Directions

1. Heat olive oil in a large skillet over medium heat.
2. Add sliced onion and minced garlic; sauté until onion is translucent.
3. Stir in chickpeas, cumin, and paprika; cook for 5 minutes.
4. Add spinach leaves and cook until wilted, about 3 minutes.
5. Season with salt, pepper, and lemon juice; stir well.
6. Serve warm and enjoy your nutritious meal.

### Nutritional Information

Calories: 210, Protein: 8g, Carbohydrates: 30g, Fat: 7g, Fiber: 8g, Cholesterol: 0mg, Sodium: 320mg, Potassium: 540mg

## SHEET PAN SALMON & VEGETABLES

**Servings 4 | Prep: 10 min | Cook: 20 min**

This vibrant and nutritious dish combines succulent salmon with a medley of colorful vegetables, all roasted to perfection on a single sheet pan for an easy and healthy meal.

### Equipment

Sheet Pan, Mixing Bowl, Oven

### Ingredients

- 1 lb salmon fillets
- 2 cups broccoli florets
- 1 cup cherry tomatoes, halved
- 1 red bell pepper, sliced
- 2 tbsp olive oil
- 1 tsp garlic powder
- 1 tsp dried oregano
- 1 lemon, sliced
- Salt and pepper to taste

### Directions

1. Preheat the oven to 400°F (200°C).
2. In a mixing bowl, toss broccoli, cherry tomatoes, and bell pepper with olive oil, garlic powder, oregano, salt, and pepper.
3. Spread the vegetables evenly on a sheet pan and place the salmon fillets on top.
4. Arrange lemon slices over the salmon and vegetables.
5. Roast in the oven for 20 minutes, or until the salmon is cooked through and vegetables are tender.
6. Remove from oven and let it rest for a few minutes before serving.

### Nutritional Information

Calories: 320, Protein: 28g, Carbohydrates: 12g, Fat: 18g, Fiber: 4g, Cholesterol: 70mg, Sodium: 220mg, Potassium: 850mg

## GARLIC BUTTER SHRIMP WITH ZOODLES

**Servings 4 | Prep: 10 min | Cook: 10 min**

This dish combines succulent shrimp with fresh zucchini noodles, all enveloped in a rich garlic butter sauce. It's a light yet satisfying meal perfect for clean eating enthusiasts.

### Equipment

Large Skillet, Spiralizer, Tongs

### Ingredients

- 1 lb large shrimp, peeled and deveined
- 2 tbsp unsalted butter
- 4 cloves garlic, minced
- 2 medium zucchinis, spiralized
- 1 tbsp lemon juice
- 1/4 tsp red pepper flakes
- Salt and pepper to taste
- 2 tbsp chopped fresh parsley

### Directions

1. Heat the butter in a large skillet over medium heat until melted.
2. Add the garlic and sauté for about 1 minute until fragrant.
3. Add the shrimp to the skillet, season with salt, pepper, and red pepper flakes, and cook for 2-3 minutes on each side until pink and opaque.
4. Stir in the lemon juice and parsley, then remove the shrimp from the skillet and set aside.
5. In the same skillet, add the spiralized zucchini and toss for 2-3 minutes until just tender.
6. Return the shrimp to the skillet, toss everything together, and serve immediately.

### Nutritional Information

Calories: 210, Protein: 25g, Carbohydrates: 6g, Fat: 10g, Fiber: 2g, Cholesterol: 170 mg, Sodium: 480 mg, Potassium: 540 mg

# SPICED TURKEY & VEGGIE SKILLET

**Servings 4 | Prep: 10 min | Cook: 20 min**

A vibrant and hearty dish, this Spiced Turkey & Veggie Skillet combines lean protein with a medley of colorful vegetables, all seasoned with warm spices for a satisfying and nutritious meal.

### Equipment

Large Skillet, Wooden Spoon, Cutting Board

### Ingredients

- 1 lb ground turkey
- 1 tbsp olive oil
- 1 cup bell peppers, diced (any color)
- 1 cup zucchini, sliced
- 1 cup cherry tomatoes, halved
- 1 tsp ground cumin
- 1 tsp smoked paprika
- 1/2 tsp garlic powder
- 1/2 tsp onion powder
- Salt and pepper to taste
- 2 tbsp fresh cilantro, chopped (optional)

### Directions

1. Heat olive oil in a large skillet over medium heat.
2. Add ground turkey, breaking it up with a wooden spoon, and cook until browned, about 5-7 minutes.
3. Stir in bell peppers, zucchini, and cherry tomatoes; cook until vegetables are tender, about 5 minutes.
4. Sprinkle cumin, smoked paprika, garlic powder, onion powder, salt, and pepper over the mixture; stir well to combine.
5. Cook for an additional 3-5 minutes, allowing flavors to meld.
6. Garnish with fresh cilantro before serving, if desired.

### Nutritional Information

Calories: 250, Protein: 28g, Carbohydrates: 10g, Fat: 12g, Fiber: 3g, Cholesterol: 70mg, Sodium: 150mg, Potassium: 600mg

# MOROCCAN CHICKPEA STEW

**Servings 4 | Prep: 15 min | Cook: 30 min**

This Moroccan Chickpea Stew is a hearty and flavorful dish, rich with spices and packed with nutritious vegetables, perfect for a warming meal.

### Equipment

Large Pot, Wooden Spoon, Knife

### Ingredients

- 1 tbsp olive oil
- 1 medium onion, chopped
- 2 cloves garlic, minced
- 1 tsp ground cumin
- 1 tsp ground coriander
- 1/2 tsp ground cinnamon
- 1/4 tsp cayenne pepper
- 1 (15 oz) can chickpeas, drained and rinsed
- 1 (14.5 oz) can diced tomatoes
- 2 cups vegetable broth
- 1 medium sweet potato, peeled and diced
- 1/2 cup dried apricots, chopped
- Salt and pepper to taste
- 1/4 cup fresh cilantro, chopped

### Directions

1. Heat olive oil in a large pot over medium heat. Add onion and garlic; sauté until onion is translucent.
2. Stir in cumin, coriander, cinnamon, and cayenne pepper; cook for 1 minute until fragrant.
3. Add chickpeas, diced tomatoes, and vegetable broth; bring to a simmer.
4. Add sweet potato and apricots; cover and cook for 20 minutes, or until sweet potatoes are tender.
5. Season with salt and pepper to taste. Stir in fresh cilantro before serving.

### Nutritional Information

Calories: 280, Protein: 8g, Carbohydrates: 50g, Fat: 6g, Fiber: 10g, Cholesterol: 0mg, Sodium: 480mg, Potassium: 780mg

# LEMON DILL GRILLED CHICKEN

**Servings 4 | Prep: 15 min | Cook: 20 min**

This Lemon Dill Grilled Chicken is a refreshing and flavorful dish, perfect for a clean eating lifestyle. The zesty lemon and fresh dill create a delightful marinade that enhances the natural taste of the chicken.

### Equipment

Grill, Mixing Bowl, Whisk

### Ingredients

- 1 lb boneless, skinless chicken breasts
- 1/4 cup fresh lemon juice
- 2 tbsp olive oil
- 2 tbsp fresh dill, chopped
- 2 cloves garlic, minced
- 1/2 tsp salt
- 1/4 tsp black pepper

### Directions

1. In a mixing bowl, whisk together lemon juice, olive oil, dill, garlic, salt, and pepper.
2. Place chicken breasts in the bowl, ensuring they are well coated with the marinade. Cover and refrigerate for at least 30 minutes.
3. Preheat the grill to medium-high heat.
4. Remove chicken from the marinade and place on the grill. Cook for 6-8 minutes on each side, or until the internal temperature reaches 165°F.
5. Let the chicken rest for a few minutes before serving.

### Nutritional Information

Calories: 210, Protein: 28g, Carbohydrates: 2g, Fat: 10g, Fiber: 0g, Cholesterol: 70mg, Sodium: 320mg, Potassium: 450mg

# MUSHROOM & LENTIL MEATBALLS

**Servings 4 | Prep: 20 min | Cook: 25 min**

These savory mushroom and lentil meatballs are a delicious plant-based alternative, packed with flavor and nutrients. Perfect for a clean eating lifestyle, they pair wonderfully with your favorite pasta or a fresh salad.

### Equipment

Food Processor, Baking Sheet, Mixing Bowl

### Ingredients

- 1 cup cooked lentils
- 8 oz mushrooms, finely chopped
- 1/2 cup breadcrumbs
- 1/4 cup grated Parmesan cheese
- 1 egg
- 2 cloves garlic, minced
- 1 tbsp olive oil
- 1 tsp dried oregano
- 1/2 tsp salt
- 1/4 tsp black pepper

### Directions

1. Preheat the oven to 375°F (190°C) and line a baking sheet with parchment paper.
2. In a food processor, pulse the cooked lentils and mushrooms until finely chopped.
3. Transfer the mixture to a mixing bowl and add breadcrumbs, Parmesan cheese, egg, garlic, olive oil, oregano, salt, and pepper. Mix until well combined.
4. Form the mixture into 1-inch meatballs and place them on the prepared baking sheet.
5. Bake for 20-25 minutes, or until the meatballs are firm and lightly browned.
6. Serve warm with your choice of sauce or as a topping for salads or pasta.

### Nutritional Information

Calories: 210, Protein: 12g, Carbohydrates: 28g, Fat: 7g, Fiber: 6g, Cholesterol: 35mg, Sodium: 320mg, Potassium: 450mg

# VEGAN TOFU & BROCCOLI STIR-FRY

**Servings 4 | Prep: 10 min | Cook: 15 min**

A vibrant and nutritious stir-fry that combines crispy tofu with fresh broccoli, all tossed in a savory sauce. Perfect for a quick and healthy dinner.

## Equipment

Large Skillet, Mixing Bowl, Spatula

## Ingredients

- 14 oz firm tofu, drained and cubed
- 2 cups broccoli florets
- 2 tbsp olive oil
- 3 tbsp soy sauce
- 1 tbsp maple syrup
- 1 tsp garlic powder
- 1 tsp ginger powder
- 1/4 cup water
- 1 tbsp cornstarch

## Directions

1. Heat 1 tbsp of olive oil in a large skillet over medium heat. Add the cubed tofu and cook until golden brown on all sides, about 8 minutes. Remove from skillet and set aside.
2. In the same skillet, add the remaining olive oil and broccoli florets. Stir-fry for 5 minutes until the broccoli is tender-crisp.
3. In a mixing bowl, whisk together soy sauce, maple syrup, garlic powder, ginger powder, water, and cornstarch until smooth.
4. Pour the sauce over the broccoli in the skillet, stirring constantly until the sauce thickens, about 2 minutes.
5. Return the tofu to the skillet, tossing to coat with the sauce. Cook for an additional 2 minutes to heat through.
6. Serve immediately, garnished with sesame seeds or green onions if desired.

## Nutritional Information

Calories: 210, Protein: 14g, Carbohydrates: 15g, Fat: 12g, Fiber: 3g, Cholesterol: 0 mg, Sodium: 620 mg, Potassium: 450 mg

# ROASTED ROOT VEGETABLE MEDLEY

**Servings 4 | Prep: 15 min | Cook: 40 min**

This vibrant Roasted Root Vegetable Medley is a celebration of earthy flavors and vibrant colors, perfect for a wholesome main dish. The natural sweetness of the vegetables is enhanced by roasting, creating a comforting and nutritious meal.

## Equipment

Baking Sheet, Mixing Bowl, Oven

## Ingredients

- 1 lb carrots, peeled and cut into 1-inch pieces
- 1 lb parsnips, peeled and cut into 1-inch pieces
- 1 lb sweet potatoes, peeled and cubed
- 2 tbsp olive oil
- 1 tsp salt
- 1/2 tsp black pepper
- 1 tsp dried thyme
- 1 tbsp fresh parsley, chopped (for garnish)

## Directions

1. Preheat the oven to 400°F (200°C).
2. In a mixing bowl, combine carrots, parsnips, and sweet potatoes.
3. Drizzle olive oil over the vegetables and sprinkle with salt, pepper, and thyme. Toss to coat evenly.
4. Spread the vegetables in a single layer on a baking sheet.
5. Roast in the oven for 35-40 minutes, stirring halfway through, until vegetables are tender and golden brown.
6. Remove from the oven and garnish with fresh parsley before serving.

## Nutritional Information

Calories: 220, Protein: 3g, Carbohydrates: 40g, Fat: 7g, Fiber: 8g, Cholesterol: 0mg, Sodium: 590mg, Potassium: 800mg

# COCONUT CURRY LENTILS

**Servings 4 | Prep: 10 min | Cook: 30 min**

This Coconut Curry Lentils dish is a comforting and flavorful main course, combining the richness of coconut milk with the warmth of curry spices. It's a perfect blend of creamy and spicy, ideal for a wholesome meal.

### Equipment

Large Pot, Wooden Spoon, Measuring Cups and Spoons

### Ingredients

- 1 cup dried lentils
- 1 tbsp coconut oil
- 1 medium onion, chopped
- 2 cloves garlic, minced
- 1 tbsp curry powder
- 1 can (14 oz) coconut milk
- 1 cup vegetable broth
- 1 tsp salt
- 1/2 tsp black pepper
- 1 tbsp fresh cilantro, chopped (optional for garnish)

### Directions

1. Rinse the lentils under cold water and set aside.
2. In a large pot, heat coconut oil over medium heat. Add onion and garlic, sauté until onion is translucent.
3. Stir in curry powder and cook for 1 minute until fragrant.
4. Add lentils, coconut milk, and vegetable broth to the pot. Stir well and bring to a boil.
5. Reduce heat to low, cover, and simmer for 25-30 minutes, or until lentils are tender.
6. Season with salt and black pepper. Adjust seasoning to taste.
7. Serve hot, garnished with fresh cilantro if desired.

### Nutritional Information

Calories: 320, Protein: 12g, Carbohydrates: 40g, Fat: 15g, Fiber: 15g, Cholesterol: 0mg, Sodium: 450mg, Potassium: 600mg

# HERB-CRUSTED WHITE FISH

**Servings 4 | Prep: 10 min | Cook: 15 min**

This herb-crusted white fish is a delightful main dish that combines a crispy, flavorful crust with tender, flaky fish. Perfect for a clean eating lifestyle, it's both nutritious and delicious.

### Equipment

Baking Sheet, Mixing Bowl, Oven

### Ingredients

- 1 lb white fish fillets (such as cod or tilapia)
- 1 cup whole wheat breadcrumbs
- 2 tbsp fresh parsley, chopped
- 1 tbsp fresh dill, chopped
- 1 tbsp lemon zest
- 1/2 tsp garlic powder
- 1/4 tsp sea salt
- 1/4 tsp black pepper
- 2 tbsp olive oil

### Directions

1. Preheat the oven to 400°F (200°C).
2. In a mixing bowl, combine breadcrumbs, parsley, dill, lemon zest, garlic powder, salt, and pepper.
3. Brush each fish fillet with olive oil and press into the breadcrumb mixture, ensuring an even coating.
4. Place the coated fillets on a baking sheet lined with parchment paper.
5. Bake in the preheated oven for 12-15 minutes, or until the fish is cooked through and the crust is golden brown.

### Nutritional Information

Calories: 250, Protein: 25g, Carbohydrates: 15g, Fat: 10g, Fiber: 2g, Cholesterol: 55mg, Sodium: 220mg, Potassium: 450mg

# Side Dishes & Vegetables

# ROASTED BRUSSELS SPROUTS WITH BALSAMIC GLAZE

**Servings 4 | Prep: 10 min | Cook: 25 min**

These roasted Brussels sprouts are perfectly caramelized and drizzled with a tangy balsamic glaze, making them a delightful and healthy side dish.

### Equipment

Baking Sheet, Mixing Bowl, Saucepan

### Ingredients

- 1 lb Brussels sprouts, trimmed and halved
- 2 tbsp olive oil
- 1/2 tsp salt
- 1/4 tsp black pepper
- 1/4 cup balsamic vinegar
- 1 tbsp honey

### Directions

1. Preheat the oven to 400°F (200°C).
2. In a mixing bowl, toss the Brussels sprouts with olive oil, salt, and pepper until evenly coated.
3. Spread the Brussels sprouts in a single layer on a baking sheet.
4. Roast in the oven for 20-25 minutes, stirring halfway through, until they are golden and tender.
5. Meanwhile, in a saucepan, combine balsamic vinegar and honey. Simmer over medium heat until reduced by half, about 5 minutes.
6. Drizzle the balsamic glaze over the roasted Brussels sprouts before serving.

### Nutritional Information

Calories: 130, Protein: 3g, Carbohydrates: 15g, Fat: 7g, Fiber: 4g, Cholesterol: 0mg, Sodium: 300mg, Potassium: 450mg

# GARLIC MASHED CAULIFLOWER

**Servings 4 | Prep: 10 min | Cook: 15 min**

A creamy and flavorful alternative to traditional mashed potatoes, this garlic mashed cauliflower is a delightful side dish that complements any meal.

### Equipment

Medium Pot, Food Processor, Mixing Bowl

### Ingredients

- 1 large head cauliflower, cut into florets
- 2 tablespoons olive oil
- 3 cloves garlic, minced
- 1/4 cup unsweetened almond milk
- 1/4 teaspoon salt
- 1/4 teaspoon black pepper
- 1 tablespoon fresh parsley, chopped (optional)

### Directions

1. Bring a medium pot of water to a boil. Add cauliflower florets and cook until tender, about 10 minutes. Drain well.
2. In a food processor, combine cooked cauliflower, olive oil, minced garlic, and almond milk. Blend until smooth and creamy.
3. Season with salt and black pepper to taste.
4. Transfer to a mixing bowl and garnish with fresh parsley if desired.
5. Serve warm as a delicious side dish.

### Nutritional Information

Calories: 110, Protein: 3g, Carbohydrates: 9g, Fat: 8g, Fiber: 4g, Cholesterol: 0mg, Sodium: 180mg, Potassium: 430mg

# SPICY ROASTED SWEET POTATOES

**Servings 4 | Prep: 10 min | Cook: 30 min**

These spicy roasted sweet potatoes are a perfect blend of heat and sweetness, making them an irresistible side dish for any meal.

### Equipment

Baking Sheet, Mixing Bowl, Oven

### Ingredients

- 2 lbs sweet potatoes, peeled and cubed
- 2 tbsp olive oil
- 1 tsp smoked paprika
- 1/2 tsp cayenne pepper
- 1 tsp garlic powder
- 1/2 tsp salt
- 1/4 tsp black pepper

### Directions

1. Preheat the oven to 400°F (200°C).
2. In a mixing bowl, combine olive oil, smoked paprika, cayenne pepper, garlic powder, salt, and black pepper.
3. Add the cubed sweet potatoes to the bowl and toss until they are evenly coated with the spice mixture.
4. Spread the sweet potatoes in a single layer on a baking sheet.
5. Roast in the preheated oven for 25-30 minutes, turning halfway through, until they are tender and slightly crispy on the edges.

### Nutritional Information

Calories: 180, Protein: 2g, Carbohydrates: 36g, Fat: 5g, Fiber: 5g, Cholesterol: 0mg, Sodium: 310mg, Potassium: 448mg

# LEMON & HERB QUINOA

**Servings 4 | Prep: 10 min | Cook: 15 min**

This vibrant and zesty quinoa dish is infused with fresh herbs and a hint of lemon, making it a perfect clean-eating side dish that pairs well with any main course.

### Equipment

Medium Saucepan, Fine Mesh Sieve, Mixing Bowl

### Ingredients

- 1 cup quinoa
- 2 cups water
- 1/4 tsp salt
- 2 tbsp fresh lemon juice
- 1 tbsp olive oil
- 1/4 cup chopped fresh parsley
- 1/4 cup chopped fresh cilantro
- 1 tsp lemon zest
- 1/4 tsp black pepper

### Directions

1. Rinse the quinoa under cold water using a fine mesh sieve.
2. In a medium saucepan, combine the quinoa, water, and salt. Bring to a boil over medium-high heat.
3. Reduce the heat to low, cover, and simmer for 15 minutes or until the quinoa is tender and water is absorbed.
4. Remove from heat and let it sit, covered, for 5 minutes. Fluff with a fork.
5. In a mixing bowl, combine the lemon juice, olive oil, parsley, cilantro, lemon zest, and black pepper.
6. Add the cooked quinoa to the bowl and toss until well combined.
7. Serve warm or at room temperature.

### Nutritional Information

Calories: 180, Protein: 6g, Carbohydrates: 30g, Fat: 5g, Fiber: 3g, Cholesterol: 0mg, Sodium: 160mg, Potassium: 320mg

# GRILLED ASPARAGUS WITH LEMON ZEST

**Servings 4 | Prep: 10 min | Cook: 8 min**

This vibrant and fresh side dish features tender grilled asparagus enhanced with the bright flavor of lemon zest, making it a perfect complement to any clean eating meal.

### Equipment

Grill, Tongs, Zester

### Ingredients

- 1 lb fresh asparagus, trimmed
- 1 tbsp olive oil
- 1 tsp lemon zest
- 1/2 tsp sea salt
- 1/4 tsp black pepper
- 1 tbsp fresh lemon juice

### Directions

1. Preheat the grill to medium-high heat.
2. Toss the asparagus with olive oil, sea salt, and black pepper in a large bowl.
3. Place the asparagus on the grill and cook for 4 minutes, turning occasionally with tongs.
4. Remove from the grill and transfer to a serving platter.
5. Sprinkle with lemon zest and drizzle with fresh lemon juice before serving.

### Nutritional Information

Calories: 60, Protein: 2g, Carbohydrates: 5g, Fat: 4g, Fiber: 2g, Cholesterol: 0mg, Sodium: 150mg, Potassium: 230mg

# SAUTÉED GARLIC KALE

**Servings 4 | Prep: 5 min | Cook: 10 min**

This vibrant and nutritious side dish features tender kale leaves infused with the rich aroma of garlic, offering a perfect balance of flavors and a delightful crunch.

### Equipment

Large Skillet, Wooden Spoon, Knife

### Ingredients

- 1 lb kale, stems removed and leaves chopped
- 2 tbsp olive oil
- 4 cloves garlic, minced
- 1/4 tsp salt
- 1/4 tsp black pepper
- 1 tbsp lemon juice

### Directions

1. Heat olive oil in a large skillet over medium heat.
2. Add minced garlic and sauté for 1 minute until fragrant.
3. Add chopped kale to the skillet, tossing to coat in the garlic oil.
4. Season with salt and black pepper, stirring occasionally for about 5-7 minutes until the kale is wilted and tender.
5. Remove from heat and drizzle with lemon juice before serving.

### Nutritional Information

Calories: 120, Protein: 3g, Carbohydrates: 8g, Fat: 9g, Fiber: 2g, Cholesterol: 0mg, Sodium: 160mg, Potassium: 450mg

# COCONUT GINGER CARROT FRIES

**Servings 4 | Prep: 10 min | Cook: 25 min**

These Coconut Ginger Carrot Fries offer a delightful twist on traditional fries, combining the natural sweetness of carrots with the aromatic flavors of coconut and ginger. Perfect as a side dish or a healthy snack.

### Equipment

Baking Sheet, Mixing Bowl, Oven

### Ingredients

- 1 lb carrots, peeled and cut into fries
- 2 tbsp coconut oil, melted
- 1 tsp fresh ginger, grated
- 1/2 tsp sea salt
- 1/4 tsp black pepper
- 1/4 cup unsweetened shredded coconut

### Directions

1. Preheat the oven to 400°F (200°C).
2. In a mixing bowl, combine the carrot fries with melted coconut oil, grated ginger, sea salt, and black pepper. Toss until well coated.
3. Spread the carrot fries in a single layer on a baking sheet.
4. Bake for 20 minutes, turning halfway through, until the carrots are tender and slightly crispy.
5. Sprinkle shredded coconut over the fries and bake for an additional 5 minutes until the coconut is lightly toasted.

### Nutritional Information

Calories: 120, Protein: 1g, Carbohydrates: 14g, Fat: 8g, Fiber: 4g, Cholesterol: 0mg, Sodium: 150mg, Potassium: 320mg

# ZUCCHINI & PARMESAN BAKE

**Servings 4 | Prep: 15 min | Cook: 25 min**

This Zucchini & Parmesan Bake is a delightful and healthy side dish that combines the freshness of zucchini with the rich flavor of Parmesan cheese. It's a perfect addition to any clean eating meal plan.

### Equipment

Oven, Baking Dish, Mixing Bowl

### Ingredients

- 2 medium zucchinis, sliced (about 1 lb)
- 1 cup grated Parmesan cheese
- 1/2 cup whole wheat breadcrumbs
- 1 tbsp olive oil
- 1 tsp garlic powder
- 1/2 tsp salt
- 1/4 tsp black pepper
- 1 tbsp fresh parsley, chopped (optional for garnish)

### Directions

1. Preheat the oven to 400°F (200°C).
2. In a mixing bowl, combine the sliced zucchinis, olive oil, garlic powder, salt, and black pepper. Toss until the zucchini slices are evenly coated.
3. In a separate bowl, mix the grated Parmesan cheese and breadcrumbs.
4. Arrange the zucchini slices in a single layer in a baking dish. Sprinkle the Parmesan and breadcrumb mixture evenly over the top.
5. Bake in the preheated oven for 20-25 minutes, or until the zucchini is tender and the top is golden brown.
6. Remove from the oven and let it cool slightly. Garnish with fresh parsley before serving, if desired.

### Nutritional Information

Calories: 180, Protein: 10g, Carbohydrates: 12g, Fat: 10g, Fiber: 3g, Cholesterol: 15mg, Sodium: 400mg, Potassium: 450mg

# ROASTED BEET & ORANGE MEDLEY

**Servings 4 | Prep: 15 min | Cook: 40 min**

This vibrant side dish combines the earthy sweetness of roasted beets with the zesty brightness of oranges, creating a delightful medley that's both refreshing and satisfying.

### Equipment

Baking Sheet, Mixing Bowl, Aluminum Foil

### Ingredients

- 1 lb beets, peeled and cut into wedges
- 2 tbsp olive oil
- 1/2 tsp salt
- 1/4 tsp black pepper
- 2 medium oranges, peeled and segmented
- 1 tbsp fresh mint, chopped
- 1 tbsp balsamic vinegar

### Directions

1. Preheat the oven to 400°F (200°C).
2. Toss the beet wedges with olive oil, salt, and black pepper in a mixing bowl.
3. Spread the beets on a baking sheet lined with aluminum foil and roast for 35-40 minutes, or until tender.
4. Once roasted, let the beets cool slightly, then combine them with orange segments in a serving bowl.
5. Drizzle with balsamic vinegar and sprinkle with fresh mint before serving.

### Nutritional Information

Calories: 160, Protein: 2g, Carbohydrates: 25g, Fat: 7g, Fiber: 5g, Cholesterol: 0mg, Sodium: 300mg, Potassium: 550mg

# TURMERIC-SPICED LENTILS

**Servings 4 | Prep: 10 min | Cook: 30 min**

A warm and nourishing side dish, these turmeric-spiced lentils are infused with aromatic spices, offering a delightful burst of flavor and a vibrant golden hue.

### Equipment

Medium saucepan, Wooden spoon, Measuring cups and spoons

### Ingredients

- 1 cup red lentils
- 2 cups water
- 1 tbsp olive oil
- 1 small onion, finely chopped
- 2 cloves garlic, minced
- 1 tsp ground turmeric
- 1 tsp ground cumin
- 1/2 tsp ground coriander
- 1/2 tsp salt
- 1/4 tsp black pepper
- 1 tbsp lemon juice
- 2 tbsp fresh cilantro, chopped (optional)

### Directions

1. Rinse the lentils under cold water until the water runs clear.
2. In a medium saucepan, heat olive oil over medium heat. Add onion and garlic, sauté until softened, about 3-4 minutes.
3. Stir in turmeric, cumin, and coriander, cooking for another minute until fragrant.
4. Add the rinsed lentils and water to the saucepan. Bring to a boil, then reduce heat to low and cover. Simmer for 20-25 minutes, or until lentils are tender.
5. Stir in salt, pepper, and lemon juice. Adjust seasoning to taste.
6. Garnish with fresh cilantro before serving, if desired.

### Nutritional Information

Calories: 180, Protein: 10g, Carbohydrates: 28g, Fat: 4g, Fiber: 10g, Cholesterol: 0mg, Sodium: 310mg, Potassium: 370mg

# HONEY ROASTED CARROTS

**Servings 4 | Prep: 10 min | Cook: 25 min**

These honey roasted carrots are a delightful blend of natural sweetness and a hint of caramelization, making them a perfect clean eating side dish.

### Equipment

Baking Sheet, Mixing Bowl, Oven

### Ingredients

- 1 lb carrots, peeled and cut into sticks
- 2 tbsp olive oil
- 2 tbsp honey
- 1 tsp salt
- 1/2 tsp black pepper
- 1 tbsp fresh thyme leaves (optional)

### Directions

1. Preheat the oven to 400°F (200°C).
2. In a mixing bowl, combine olive oil, honey, salt, and black pepper.
3. Add the carrot sticks to the bowl and toss until they are evenly coated with the mixture.
4. Spread the carrots in a single layer on a baking sheet.
5. Roast in the preheated oven for 20-25 minutes, or until the carrots are tender and slightly caramelized.
6. Sprinkle fresh thyme leaves over the roasted carrots before serving, if desired.

### Nutritional Information

Calories: 130, Protein: 1g, Carbohydrates: 19g, Fat: 7g, Fiber: 3g, Cholesterol: 0mg, Sodium: 590mg, Potassium: 400mg

# CUMIN-SPICED CHICKPEAS

**Servings 4 | Prep: 10 min | Cook: 15 min**

A delightful and aromatic side dish, these cumin-spiced chickpeas are packed with flavor and nutrition, perfect for complementing any meal with a touch of warmth and spice.

### Equipment

Skillet, Mixing Spoon, Measuring Spoons

### Ingredients

- 2 tbsp olive oil
- 1 tsp cumin seeds
- 1 can (15 oz) chickpeas, drained and rinsed
- 1/2 tsp smoked paprika
- 1/4 tsp cayenne pepper (optional)
- 1/2 tsp sea salt
- 1 tbsp lemon juice
- 2 tbsp fresh cilantro, chopped

### Directions

1. Heat olive oil in a skillet over medium heat.
2. Add cumin seeds and sauté until fragrant, about 1 minute.
3. Stir in chickpeas, smoked paprika, cayenne pepper, and sea salt. Cook for 10 minutes, stirring occasionally.
4. Remove from heat and drizzle with lemon juice.
5. Garnish with fresh cilantro before serving.

### Nutritional Information

Calories: 180, Protein: 6g, Carbohydrates: 20g, Fat: 9g, Fiber: 6g, Cholesterol: 0mg, Sodium: 300mg, Potassium: 200mg

# QUINOA & HERB PILAF

**Servings 4 | Prep: 10 min | Cook: 20 min**

This Quinoa & Herb Pilaf is a delightful, nutrient-packed side dish that combines fluffy quinoa with fresh herbs, offering a burst of flavor and a perfect complement to any main course.

### Equipment

Medium Saucepan, Fine Mesh Strainer, Wooden Spoon

### Ingredients

- 1 cup quinoa
- 2 cups water
- 1 tbsp olive oil
- 1/2 cup chopped onion
- 1/4 cup chopped fresh parsley
- 1/4 cup chopped fresh cilantro
- 1 tsp salt
- 1/2 tsp black pepper
- 1 tbsp lemon juice

### Directions

1. Rinse the quinoa under cold water using a fine mesh strainer.
2. In a medium saucepan, heat olive oil over medium heat and sauté the chopped onion until translucent.
3. Add the rinsed quinoa to the saucepan and toast for 2 minutes, stirring frequently.
4. Pour in the water, add salt and pepper, and bring to a boil. Reduce heat to low, cover, and simmer for 15 minutes or until the quinoa is tender and water is absorbed.
5. Remove from heat and let it sit, covered, for 5 minutes. Fluff with a fork.
6. Stir in the chopped parsley, cilantro, and lemon juice. Adjust seasoning if necessary.

### Nutritional Information

Calories: 180, Protein: 6g, Carbohydrates: 30g, Fat: 5g, Fiber: 4g, Cholesterol: 0mg, Sodium: 300mg, Potassium: 220mg

# BALSAMIC ROASTED MUSHROOMS

**Servings 4 | Prep: 10 min | Cook: 20 min**

These balsamic roasted mushrooms are a savory delight, offering a perfect blend of tangy and earthy flavors. Ideal as a side dish or a topping for salads and grain bowls.

### Equipment

Baking Sheet, Mixing Bowl, Oven

### Ingredients

- 16 oz cremini mushrooms, cleaned and halved
- 2 tbsp balsamic vinegar
- 1 tbsp olive oil
- 2 cloves garlic, minced
- 1 tsp dried thyme
- 1/2 tsp salt
- 1/4 tsp black pepper

### Directions

1. Preheat the oven to 400°F (200°C).
2. In a mixing bowl, combine balsamic vinegar, olive oil, minced garlic, dried thyme, salt, and black pepper.
3. Add the halved mushrooms to the bowl and toss until they are evenly coated with the mixture.
4. Spread the mushrooms in a single layer on a baking sheet.
5. Roast in the preheated oven for 20 minutes, stirring halfway through, until mushrooms are tender and caramelized.

### Nutritional Information

Calories: 70, Protein: 3g, Carbohydrates: 7g, Fat: 4g, Fiber: 1g, Cholesterol: 0mg, Sodium: 310mg, Potassium: 390mg

# SPAGHETTI SQUASH WITH PESTO

**Servings 4 | Prep: 10 min | Cook: 40 min**

This delightful dish combines the nutty flavor of spaghetti squash with the fresh, vibrant taste of homemade pesto, creating a satisfying and healthy side dish.

### Equipment

Oven, Baking Sheet, Fork, Blender or Food Processor

### Ingredients

- 1 medium spaghetti squash (about 3 lbs)
- 2 tbsp olive oil
- 1 cup fresh basil leaves
- 1/4 cup pine nuts
- 1/4 cup grated Parmesan cheese
- 2 cloves garlic
- 1/4 cup olive oil (for pesto)
- Salt and pepper to taste

### Directions

1. Preheat the oven to 400°F (200°C). Cut the spaghetti squash in half lengthwise and remove the seeds.
2. Drizzle the squash halves with 2 tbsp olive oil, season with salt and pepper, and place cut-side down on a baking sheet.
3. Roast in the oven for 35-40 minutes until the flesh is tender and easily shredded with a fork.
4. While the squash is roasting, prepare the pesto by blending basil, pine nuts, Parmesan, garlic, and 1/4 cup olive oil in a blender or food processor until smooth.
5. Once the squash is cooked, use a fork to scrape out the strands into a bowl.
6. Toss the spaghetti squash with the prepared pesto until well combined.
7. Serve warm, garnished with additional Parmesan if desired.

### Nutritional Information

Calories: 250, Protein: 5g, Carbohydrates: 20g, Fat: 18g, Fiber: 4g, Cholesterol: 5mg, Sodium: 150mg, Potassium: 450mg

# AVOCADO & TOMATO SALSA

**Servings 4 | Prep: 10 min | Cook: 0 min**

This vibrant and refreshing salsa combines creamy avocado with juicy tomatoes, making it a perfect clean-eating side dish or topping for your favorite meals.

### Equipment

Cutting Board, Knife, Mixing Bowl, Spoon

### Ingredients

- 2 medium avocados, diced
- 1 cup cherry tomatoes, quartered
- 1/4 cup red onion, finely chopped
- 1/4 cup fresh cilantro, chopped
- 1 tablespoon lime juice
- 1/2 teaspoon sea salt
- 1/4 teaspoon black pepper

### Directions

1. In a mixing bowl, combine the diced avocados and quartered cherry tomatoes.
2. Add the finely chopped red onion and fresh cilantro to the bowl.
3. Drizzle the lime juice over the mixture and season with sea salt and black pepper.
4. Gently toss all ingredients together until well combined.
5. Serve immediately or refrigerate for up to 1 hour to let the flavors meld.

### Nutritional Information

Calories: 150, Protein: 2g, Carbohydrates: 12g, Fat: 11g, Fiber: 6g, Cholesterol: 0mg, Sodium: 150mg, Potassium: 500mg

# SAUTÉED GREEN BEANS WITH ALMONDS

**Servings 4 | Prep: 10 min | Cook: 10 min**

A delightful and crunchy side dish, these sautéed green beans with almonds offer a perfect blend of freshness and nuttiness, making them an ideal accompaniment to any clean eating meal.

### Equipment

Skillet, Spatula, Measuring Cups

### Ingredients

- 1 lb fresh green beans, trimmed
- 2 tbsp olive oil
- 1/4 cup sliced almonds
- 2 cloves garlic, minced
- 1/2 tsp salt
- 1/4 tsp black pepper
- 1 tbsp lemon juice

### Directions

1. Heat olive oil in a skillet over medium heat.
2. Add the green beans and sauté for 5 minutes, stirring occasionally.
3. Stir in the garlic and sliced almonds, cooking for an additional 3 minutes until the almonds are lightly toasted.
4. Season with salt and black pepper, mixing well.
5. Drizzle with lemon juice, toss to combine, and serve warm.

### Nutritional Information

Calories: 150, Protein: 3g, Carbohydrates: 10g, Fat: 12g, Fiber: 4g, Cholesterol: 0mg, Sodium: 300mg, Potassium: 250mg

# CINNAMON ROASTED BUTTERNUT SQUASH

**Servings 4 | Prep: 10 min | Cook: 30 min**

This delightful side dish combines the natural sweetness of butternut squash with the warm, comforting aroma of cinnamon, making it a perfect addition to any clean eating meal.

### Equipment

Baking Sheet, Mixing Bowl, Oven

### Ingredients

- 2 lbs butternut squash, peeled and cubed
- 2 tbsp olive oil
- 1 tsp ground cinnamon
- 1/2 tsp sea salt
- 1/4 tsp black pepper

### Directions

1. Preheat the oven to 400°F (200°C).
2. In a mixing bowl, combine the cubed butternut squash, olive oil, cinnamon, sea salt, and black pepper. Toss until the squash is evenly coated.
3. Spread the squash in a single layer on a baking sheet.
4. Roast in the preheated oven for 25-30 minutes, stirring halfway through, until the squash is tender and lightly caramelized.
5. Remove from the oven and serve warm.

### Nutritional Information

Calories: 150, Protein: 2g, Carbohydrates: 28g, Fat: 7g, Fiber: 4g, Cholesterol: 0mg, Sodium: 300mg, Potassium: 600mg

# SWEET CORN & BLACK BEAN SALAD

**Servings 4 | Prep: 15 min | Cook: 0 min**

This vibrant and refreshing salad combines the sweetness of corn with the earthiness of black beans, creating a perfect side dish that complements any meal.

### Equipment

Mixing Bowl, Measuring Cups, Spoon

### Ingredients

- 1 cup sweet corn kernels (fresh or frozen, thawed)
- 1 cup canned black beans, rinsed and drained
- 1/2 cup cherry tomatoes, halved
- 1/4 cup red onion, finely chopped
- 1/4 cup cilantro, chopped
- 2 tbsp lime juice
- 1 tbsp olive oil
- 1/2 tsp salt
- 1/4 tsp black pepper

### Directions

1. In a mixing bowl, combine the sweet corn, black beans, cherry tomatoes, red onion, and cilantro.
2. In a small bowl, whisk together lime juice, olive oil, salt, and black pepper.
3. Pour the dressing over the salad ingredients and toss gently to combine.
4. Let the salad sit for 5 minutes to allow flavors to meld.
5. Serve chilled or at room temperature.

### Nutritional Information

Calories: 150, Protein: 5g, Carbohydrates: 25g, Fat: 5g, Fiber: 7g, Cholesterol: 0mg, Sodium: 300mg, Potassium: 400mg

# MISO GLAZED EGGPLANT

**Servings 4 | Prep: 10 min | Cook: 20 min**

This dish features tender eggplant with a savory-sweet miso glaze, offering a delightful umami flavor that pairs perfectly with any main course.

### Equipment

Baking Sheet, Mixing Bowl, Basting Brush

### Ingredients

- 2 medium eggplants (about 1 lb each)
- 3 tbsp white miso paste
- 2 tbsp maple syrup
- 2 tbsp soy sauce
- 1 tbsp rice vinegar
- 1 tbsp sesame oil
- 1 tsp grated fresh ginger
- 1 tbsp sesame seeds (optional, for garnish)
- 2 tbsp chopped green onions (optional, for garnish)

### Directions

1. Preheat the oven to 400°F (200°C). Line a baking sheet with parchment paper.
2. Slice the eggplants in half lengthwise and score the flesh in a crisscross pattern, being careful not to cut through the skin.
3. In a mixing bowl, combine the miso paste, maple syrup, soy sauce, rice vinegar, sesame oil, and ginger to create the glaze.
4. Brush the glaze generously over the cut sides of the eggplants.
5. Place the eggplants cut side up on the prepared baking sheet and roast for 20 minutes, or until the eggplants are tender and the glaze is caramelized.
6. Garnish with sesame seeds and green onions before serving, if desired.

### Nutritional Information

Calories: 150, Protein: 3g, Carbohydrates: 25g, Fat: 5g, Fiber: 7g, Cholesterol: 0mg, Sodium: 450mg, Potassium: 500mg

## CARROT & GINGER SLAW

**Servings 4 | Prep: 15 min | Cook: 0 min**

A refreshing and zesty slaw that combines the natural sweetness of carrots with the spicy kick of ginger, perfect as a side dish to brighten up any meal.

### Equipment

Box Grater, Mixing Bowl, Whisk

### Ingredients

- 3 cups shredded carrots
- 1 tbsp fresh ginger, grated
- 2 tbsp apple cider vinegar
- 1 tbsp olive oil
- 1 tbsp honey
- 1/4 tsp salt
- 1/4 tsp black pepper
- 2 tbsp chopped fresh cilantro

### Directions

1. In a mixing bowl, combine the shredded carrots and grated ginger.
2. In a separate small bowl, whisk together the apple cider vinegar, olive oil, honey, salt, and black pepper until well combined.
3. Pour the dressing over the carrot and ginger mixture, tossing to coat evenly.
4. Add the chopped cilantro and gently mix until distributed throughout the slaw.
5. Serve immediately or refrigerate for up to 2 hours to allow flavors to meld.

### Nutritional Information

Calories: 110, Protein: 1g, Carbohydrates: 15g, Fat: 6g, Fiber: 3g, Cholesterol: 0mg, Sodium: 150mg, Potassium: 320mg

## STEAMED BROCCOLI WITH GARLIC

**Servings 4 | Prep: 5 min | Cook: 10 min**

This simple yet flavorful dish highlights the natural goodness of broccoli, enhanced with the aromatic touch of garlic. Perfect as a nutritious side dish for any meal.

### Equipment

Steamer Basket, Saucepan, Skillet

### Ingredients

- 1 lb broccoli florets
- 2 tbsp olive oil
- 3 cloves garlic, minced
- 1/4 tsp salt
- 1/4 tsp black pepper
- 1 tbsp lemon juice

### Directions

1. Fill a saucepan with about 1 inch of water and bring to a boil. Place the steamer basket over the saucepan.
2. Add the broccoli florets to the steamer basket, cover, and steam for 5-7 minutes until tender but still bright green.
3. In a skillet, heat olive oil over medium heat. Add minced garlic and sauté for 1-2 minutes until fragrant.
4. Remove the steamed broccoli from the basket and add it to the skillet. Toss with garlic, salt, and black pepper.
5. Drizzle with lemon juice, toss again, and serve warm.

### Nutritional Information

Calories: 110, Protein: 3g, Carbohydrates: 9g, Fat: 8g, Fiber: 4g, Cholesterol: 0mg, Sodium: 160mg, Potassium: 400mg

# LEMON & HERB ROASTED CAULIFLOWER

**Servings 4 | Prep: 10 min | Cook: 25 min**

This vibrant and zesty roasted cauliflower dish is infused with fresh herbs and a hint of lemon, making it a perfect clean eating side dish that's both flavorful and nutritious.

### Equipment

Baking Sheet, Mixing Bowl, Oven

### Ingredients

- 1 medium head cauliflower, cut into florets (about 1.5 lbs)
- 2 tbsp olive oil
- 1 lemon, zested and juiced
- 2 tsp fresh thyme leaves
- 1 tsp garlic powder
- 1/2 tsp salt
- 1/4 tsp black pepper

### Directions

1. Preheat the oven to 400°F (200°C).
2. In a mixing bowl, combine olive oil, lemon zest, lemon juice, thyme, garlic powder, salt, and pepper.
3. Add cauliflower florets to the bowl and toss until evenly coated with the lemon-herb mixture.
4. Spread the cauliflower in a single layer on a baking sheet.
5. Roast in the preheated oven for 25 minutes, or until the cauliflower is tender and golden brown, stirring halfway through.
6. Serve warm, garnished with additional thyme if desired.

### Nutritional Information

Calories: 110, Protein: 3g, Carbohydrates: 10g, Fat: 7g, Fiber: 4g, Cholesterol: 0mg, Sodium: 310mg, Potassium: 450mg

# MANGO & CUCUMBER SALSA

**Servings 4 | Prep: 15 min | Cook: 0 min**

This refreshing Mango & Cucumber Salsa is a vibrant blend of sweet and tangy flavors, perfect as a side dish or a topping for grilled proteins.

### Equipment

Cutting Board, Knife, Mixing Bowl

### Ingredients

- 1 cup diced mango (about 1 medium mango)
- 1 cup diced cucumber (about 1 medium cucumber)
- 1/4 cup finely chopped red onion
- 1/4 cup chopped fresh cilantro
- 1 tbsp lime juice
- 1/2 tsp salt
- 1/4 tsp black pepper

### Directions

1. Dice the mango and cucumber into small, even pieces and place them in a mixing bowl.
2. Add the finely chopped red onion and fresh cilantro to the bowl.
3. Drizzle the lime juice over the mixture.
4. Season with salt and black pepper.
5. Gently toss all ingredients together until well combined.
6. Let the salsa sit for a few minutes to allow the flavors to meld.
7. Serve immediately or refrigerate for up to 2 hours before serving.

### Nutritional Information

Calories: 60, Protein: 1g, Carbohydrates: 15g, Fat: 0g, Fiber: 2g, Cholesterol: 0mg, Sodium: 300mg, Potassium: 180mg

# DILL & LEMON CUCUMBER SALAD

**Servings 4 | Prep: 10 min | Cook: 0 min**

A refreshing and crisp salad that combines the coolness of cucumbers with the zesty brightness of lemon and the aromatic touch of dill. Perfect as a light side dish for any meal.

### Equipment

Cutting Board, Knife, Mixing Bowl

### Ingredients

- 2 large cucumbers, thinly sliced
- 2 tbsp fresh dill, chopped
- 1 lemon, juiced
- 1 tbsp olive oil
- 1/2 tsp salt
- 1/4 tsp black pepper

### Directions

1. Slice the cucumbers thinly and place them in a mixing bowl.
2. Add the chopped dill to the cucumbers.
3. In a small bowl, whisk together the lemon juice, olive oil, salt, and black pepper.
4. Pour the dressing over the cucumbers and dill, tossing gently to combine.
5. Serve immediately or refrigerate for up to 1 hour to allow flavors to meld.

### Nutritional Information

Calories: 60, Protein: 1g, Carbohydrates: 7g, Fat: 4g, Fiber: 1g, Cholesterol: 0mg, Sodium: 300mg, Potassium: 250mg

# HERB-INFUSED BROWN RICE

**Servings 4 | Prep: 5 min | Cook: 45 min**

This herb-infused brown rice is a fragrant and flavorful side dish, perfect for complementing any main course. The aromatic herbs elevate the nutty taste of brown rice, making it a delightful addition to your clean eating menu.

### Equipment

Medium Saucepan, Measuring Cups, Wooden Spoon

### Ingredients

- 1 cup Brown Rice
- 2 cups Water
- 1 tbsp Olive Oil
- 1 tsp Dried Thyme
- 1 tsp Dried Rosemary
- 1/2 tsp Salt
- 1/4 tsp Black Pepper
- 1 tbsp Fresh Parsley, chopped (optional for garnish)

### Directions

1. Rinse the brown rice under cold water until the water runs clear.
2. In a medium saucepan, combine the rinsed rice, water, olive oil, dried thyme, dried rosemary, salt, and black pepper.
3. Bring the mixture to a boil over medium-high heat.
4. Once boiling, reduce the heat to low, cover the saucepan, and let it simmer for 40-45 minutes, or until the rice is tender and the water is absorbed.
5. Remove from heat and let it sit, covered, for 5 minutes. Fluff with a fork before serving.
6. Garnish with fresh parsley if desired.

### Nutritional Information

Calories: 180, Protein: 4g, Carbohydrates: 36g, Fat: 3g, Fiber: 2g, Cholesterol: 0mg, Sodium: 150mg, Potassium: 115mg

# Healthy Drinks & Tonics

# TURMERIC & GINGER GOLDEN MILK

**Servings 2 | Prep: 5 min | Cook: 10 min**

This soothing and warming drink combines the anti-inflammatory properties of turmeric and ginger with the creamy richness of almond milk, making it a perfect evening tonic.

### Equipment

Saucepan, Whisk, Measuring Cups and Spoons

### Ingredients

- 2 cups unsweetened almond milk
- 1 tsp ground turmeric
- 1/2 tsp ground ginger
- 1 tbsp honey or maple syrup
- 1/2 tsp vanilla extract
- 1/4 tsp ground cinnamon
- Pinch of black pepper

### Directions

1. In a saucepan, combine almond milk, turmeric, ginger, cinnamon, and black pepper.
2. Heat over medium heat, whisking frequently, until the mixture is hot but not boiling.
3. Remove from heat and stir in honey and vanilla extract.
4. Pour into mugs and enjoy warm.
5. Optionally, garnish with a sprinkle of cinnamon on top.

### Nutritional Information

Calories: 90, Protein: 1g, Carbohydrates: 16g, Fat: 2g, Fiber: 1g, Cholesterol: 0mg, Sodium: 150mg, Potassium: 150mg

# MATCHA GREEN TEA LATTE

**Servings 2 | Prep: 5 min | Cook: 5 min**

A soothing and invigorating drink, the Matcha Green Tea Latte combines the earthy richness of matcha with the creamy smoothness of milk, offering a perfect balance of flavor and health benefits.

### Equipment

Small saucepan, Whisk, Mug

### Ingredients

- 1 cup water
- 1 tsp matcha green tea powder
- 1 cup unsweetened almond milk (or milk of choice)
- 1 tbsp honey (or sweetener of choice)
- 1/2 tsp vanilla extract

### Directions

1. Heat the water in a small saucepan until it is just about to boil.
2. Whisk in the matcha green tea powder until fully dissolved and smooth.
3. Add the almond milk to the saucepan and heat gently, stirring occasionally.
4. Stir in the honey and vanilla extract until well combined.
5. Pour the latte into mugs and enjoy warm.

### Nutritional Information

Calories: 70, Protein: 1g, Carbohydrates: 14g, Fat: 2g, Fiber: 1g, Cholesterol: 0mg, Sodium: 80mg, Potassium: 120mg

# DETOX LEMON & CUCUMBER WATER

**Servings 4 | Prep: 10 min | Cook: 0 min**

This refreshing detox water combines the zesty flavor of lemon with the coolness of cucumber, making it a perfect hydrating drink to cleanse and rejuvenate your body.

### Equipment

Pitcher, Knife, Cutting Board

### Ingredients

- 1 medium lemon, thinly sliced
- 1/2 medium cucumber, thinly sliced
- 8 cups cold water
- 10 fresh mint leaves
- 1 teaspoon grated ginger (optional)

### Directions

1. Place the lemon and cucumber slices into the pitcher.
2. Add the fresh mint leaves and grated ginger, if using.
3. Pour the cold water over the ingredients in the pitcher.
4. Stir gently to combine all the flavors.
5. Refrigerate for at least 2 hours to allow the flavors to infuse.
6. Serve chilled, over ice if desired.

### Nutritional Information

Calories: 5, Protein: 0g, Carbohydrates: 1g, Fat: 0g, Fiber: 0g, Cholesterol: 0mg, Sodium: 2mg, Potassium: 20mg

# BERRY ANTIOXIDANT SMOOTHIE

**Servings 2 | Prep: 5 min | Cook: 0 min**

This vibrant Berry Antioxidant Smoothie is a refreshing blend of nutrient-rich berries and creamy yogurt, perfect for a quick breakfast or a revitalizing snack.

### Equipment

Blender, Measuring Cups, Measuring Spoons

### Ingredients

- 1 cup mixed berries (strawberries, blueberries, raspberries)
- 1 banana, sliced
- 1/2 cup Greek yogurt
- 1/2 cup almond milk
- 1 tbsp honey (optional)
- 1 tsp chia seeds

### Directions

1. Combine mixed berries, banana, Greek yogurt, and almond milk in a blender.
2. Blend on high speed until smooth and creamy.
3. Add honey and chia seeds, then blend again for a few seconds to incorporate.
4. Pour into glasses and serve immediately.
5. Enjoy your nutrient-packed smoothie!

### Nutritional Information

Calories: 180, Protein: 6g, Carbohydrates: 35g, Fat: 3g, Fiber: 6g, Cholesterol: 5mg, Sodium: 50mg, Potassium: 450mg

## GINGER & HONEY IMMUNITY SHOT

**Servings 4 | Prep: 10 min | Cook: 0 min**

This invigorating shot combines the warmth of ginger with the natural sweetness of honey, offering a quick boost to your immune system. Perfect for starting your day or as a midday pick-me-up.

### Equipment

Blender, Fine Mesh Strainer, Measuring Spoons

### Ingredients

- 2 oz fresh ginger root, peeled and chopped
- 1/4 cup fresh lemon juice (about 2 lemons)
- 2 tbsp raw honey
- 1/2 cup water
- 1/4 tsp cayenne pepper (optional)

### Directions

1. Combine the chopped ginger, lemon juice, honey, and water in a blender.
2. Blend on high until the mixture is smooth.
3. Strain the mixture through a fine mesh strainer into a bowl, pressing down to extract all the liquid.
4. Stir in the cayenne pepper, if using, for an extra kick.
5. Divide the shot into four small glasses and serve immediately.

### Nutritional Information

Calories: 35, Protein: 0g, Carbohydrates: 9g, Fat: 0g, Fiber: 0g, Cholesterol: 0mg, Sodium: 1mg, Potassium: 30mg

## MINT & WATERMELON REFRESHER

**Servings 4 | Prep: 10 min | Cook: 0 min**

This invigorating Mint & Watermelon Refresher is a perfect blend of juicy watermelon and fresh mint, offering a hydrating and revitalizing drink that's perfect for hot summer days.

### Equipment

Blender, Strainer, Pitcher

### Ingredients

- 4 cups watermelon, cubed
- 1/4 cup fresh mint leaves
- 1 tbsp lime juice
- 1 cup cold water
- 1 tbsp honey (optional)
- Ice cubes, as needed

### Directions

1. Combine the watermelon cubes and mint leaves in a blender.
2. Add lime juice and cold water to the blender.
3. Blend until smooth and well combined.
4. Strain the mixture through a strainer into a pitcher to remove pulp.
5. Stir in honey if desired, and serve over ice cubes.

### Nutritional Information

Calories: 60, Protein: 1g, Carbohydrates: 15g, Fat: 0g, Fiber: 1g, Cholesterol: 0mg, Sodium: 2mg, Potassium: 170mg

# ALMOND CHAI SPICED TEA

**Servings 4 | Prep: 5 min | Cook: 10 min**

This Almond Chai Spiced Tea is a warm, aromatic blend that combines the richness of almond milk with the exotic flavors of chai spices. Perfect for a cozy afternoon or a soothing evening ritual.

### Equipment

Medium Saucepan, Whisk, Strainer

### Ingredients

- 4 cups almond milk
- 2 tbsp loose leaf black tea or 4 black tea bags
- 1 tbsp honey or maple syrup
- 1 tsp ground cinnamon
- 1/2 tsp ground ginger
- 1/4 tsp ground cardamom
- 1/4 tsp ground cloves
- 1/4 tsp ground nutmeg
- 1/2 tsp vanilla extract

### Directions

1. In a medium saucepan, combine almond milk, cinnamon, ginger, cardamom, cloves, and nutmeg.
2. Heat over medium heat until the mixture begins to simmer, stirring occasionally.
3. Add the black tea and simmer for an additional 5 minutes.
4. Remove from heat and stir in honey and vanilla extract.
5. Strain the tea into cups to remove the tea leaves or bags.
6. Serve hot and enjoy the comforting blend of spices.

### Nutritional Information

Calories: 60, Protein: 1g, Carbohydrates: 10g, Fat: 2g, Fiber: 1g, Cholesterol: 0mg, Sodium: 150mg, Potassium: 180mg

# CINNAMON-SPICED APPLE CIDER

**Servings 4 | Prep: 10 min | Cook: 20 min**

Warm up with this aromatic and comforting cinnamon-spiced apple cider, perfect for cozy evenings or festive gatherings.

### Equipment

Medium Saucepan, Wooden Spoon, Fine Mesh Strainer

### Ingredients

- 4 cups apple cider
- 2 cinnamon sticks
- 1 tablespoon whole cloves
- 1 teaspoon allspice berries
- 1 orange, sliced
- 1 tablespoon honey (optional)

### Directions

1. In a medium saucepan, combine apple cider, cinnamon sticks, cloves, and allspice berries.
2. Add the orange slices to the mixture.
3. Bring the mixture to a simmer over medium heat, stirring occasionally.
4. Reduce heat to low and let it simmer for 15 minutes to allow flavors to meld.
5. Strain the cider through a fine mesh strainer to remove spices and orange slices.
6. Stir in honey, if desired, and serve warm.

### Nutritional Information

Calories: 120, Protein: 0g, Carbohydrates: 30g, Fat: 0g, Fiber: 2g, Cholesterol: 0mg, Sodium: 10mg, Potassium: 250mg

# COCONUT WATER & LIME COOLER

**Servings 2 | Prep: 10 min | Cook: 0 min**

This refreshing Coconut Water & Lime Cooler is the perfect hydrating drink, combining the natural sweetness of coconut water with a zesty lime twist. Ideal for a hot day or post-workout refreshment.

### Equipment

Blender, Citrus Juicer, Measuring Cups

### Ingredients

- 16 oz coconut water
- 2 tbsp fresh lime juice
- 1 tbsp honey (optional)
- 1/4 cup fresh mint leaves
- Ice cubes (as needed)

### Directions

1. In a blender, combine the coconut water, fresh lime juice, honey, and mint leaves.
2. Blend on high until the mint leaves are finely chopped and the mixture is well combined.
3. Fill two glasses with ice cubes.
4. Pour the cooler mixture over the ice in each glass.
5. Garnish with additional mint leaves or a lime wedge, if desired.

### Nutritional Information

Calories: 60, Protein: 0g, Carbohydrates: 16g, Fat: 0g, Fiber: 1g, Cholesterol: 0mg, Sodium: 60mg, Potassium: 400mg

# GREEN APPLE & SPINACH JUICE

**Servings 2 | Prep: 10 min | Cook: 0 min**

This refreshing juice combines the crisp sweetness of green apples with the nutrient-rich goodness of spinach, creating a revitalizing drink perfect for any time of the day.

### Equipment

Juicer, Knife, Cutting Board

### Ingredients

- 2 medium green apples, cored and chopped
- 2 cups fresh spinach leaves
- 1/2 lemon, peeled
- 1-inch piece of ginger, peeled
- 1/2 cup water

### Directions

1. Wash all produce thoroughly under running water.
2. Core and chop the green apples into manageable pieces.
3. Feed the spinach, apples, lemon, and ginger through the juicer.
4. Add water to the juice and stir well to combine.
5. Serve immediately over ice, if desired.

### Nutritional Information

Calories: 95, Protein: 1g, Carbohydrates: 24g, Fat: 0g, Fiber: 4g, Cholesterol: 0mg, Sodium: 10mg, Potassium: 350mg

# HIBISCUS & ROSEHIP VITAMIN C TEA

**Servings 4 | Prep: 5 min | Cook: 10 min**

This vibrant and tangy tea is packed with vitamin C, offering a refreshing boost to your immune system. Perfect for a soothing afternoon break or a revitalizing morning start.

### Equipment

Medium Saucepan, Strainer, Teapot or Pitcher

### Ingredients

- 4 cups water
- 2 tbsp dried hibiscus flowers
- 1 tbsp dried rosehips
- 1 tbsp honey (optional)
- 1 tsp fresh lemon juice

### Directions

1. Bring the water to a boil in a medium saucepan.
2. Add the dried hibiscus flowers and rosehips to the boiling water.
3. Reduce the heat and let it simmer for 10 minutes.
4. Strain the tea into a teapot or pitcher, discarding the solids.
5. Stir in honey and lemon juice, if desired, and serve warm or chilled.

### Nutritional Information

Calories: 20, Protein: 0g, Carbohydrates: 5g, Fat: 0g, Fiber: 0g, Cholesterol: 0mg, Sodium: 5mg, Potassium: 10mg

# ALOE VERA & LEMON HYDRATION DRINK

**Servings 2 | Prep: 10 min | Cook: 0 min**

This refreshing Aloe Vera & Lemon Hydration Drink is perfect for revitalizing your body and mind. Packed with natural electrolytes and a zesty citrus kick, it's the ideal beverage for a clean eating lifestyle.

### Equipment

Blender, Measuring Cups, Knife

### Ingredients

- 1/4 cup Aloe Vera Gel (fresh or store-bought)
- 1 Lemon, juiced
- 2 cups Cold Water
- 1 tbsp Honey (optional)
- 1/4 tsp Sea Salt
- Ice Cubes (as needed)

### Directions

1. Combine the aloe vera gel, lemon juice, cold water, honey, and sea salt in a blender.
2. Blend on high speed until the mixture is smooth and well combined.
3. Taste and adjust sweetness with more honey if desired.
4. Pour the drink into glasses filled with ice cubes.
5. Serve immediately for maximum freshness and hydration.

### Nutritional Information

Calories: 35, Protein: 0g, Carbohydrates: 9g, Fat: 0g, Fiber: 0g, Cholesterol: 0mg, Sodium: 150mg, Potassium: 50mg

# GOLDEN TURMERIC DETOX TEA

**Servings 2 | Prep: 5 min | Cook: 10 min**

This soothing and invigorating tea combines the anti-inflammatory properties of turmeric with the cleansing benefits of lemon and ginger, making it a perfect detoxifying drink.

### Equipment

Medium Saucepan, Whisk, Fine Mesh Strainer

### Ingredients

- 2 cups water
- 1 tsp ground turmeric
- 1/2 tsp ground ginger
- 1 tbsp honey
- 1 tbsp lemon juice
- 1/4 tsp black pepper

### Directions

1. In a medium saucepan, bring water to a gentle boil.
2. Add turmeric, ginger, and black pepper to the boiling water.
3. Reduce heat and let it simmer for 5 minutes, stirring occasionally.
4. Remove from heat and strain the tea into cups using a fine mesh strainer.
5. Stir in honey and lemon juice until well combined.
6. Serve warm and enjoy the detoxifying benefits.

### Nutritional Information

Calories: 35, Protein: 0g, Carbohydrates: 9g, Fat: 0g, Fiber: 0g, Cholesterol: 0mg, Sodium: 2mg, Potassium: 20mg

# COCONUT MATCHA ENERGY BOOST

**Servings 2 | Prep: 5 min | Cook: 0 min**

This invigorating drink combines the creamy richness of coconut milk with the earthy tones of matcha, providing a natural energy lift and a refreshing taste. Perfect for a morning boost or an afternoon pick-me-up.

### Equipment

Blender, Measuring Cups, Teaspoon

### Ingredients

- 1 cup coconut milk
- 1 tsp matcha powder
- 1 tbsp honey (or maple syrup for a vegan option)
- 1/2 tsp vanilla extract
- 1/2 cup ice cubes

### Directions

1. Add coconut milk, matcha powder, honey, and vanilla extract to the blender.
2. Blend on high until the mixture is smooth and well combined.
3. Add ice cubes and blend again until the ice is crushed and the drink is frothy.
4. Pour into glasses and serve immediately.
5. Optional: Garnish with a sprinkle of matcha powder on top for extra flair.

### Nutritional Information

Calories: 150, Protein: 2g, Carbohydrates: 18g, Fat: 8g, Fiber: 1g, Cholesterol: 0mg, Sodium: 20mg, Potassium: 220mg

# BLUEBERRY & ACAI ANTIOXIDANT SMOOTHIE

**Servings 2 | Prep: 5 min | Cook: 0 min**

This vibrant smoothie is packed with antioxidants, offering a refreshing and nutritious boost to your day. The combination of blueberries and acai creates a deliciously fruity and energizing drink.

### Equipment

Blender, Measuring Cups, Measuring Spoons

### Ingredients

- 1 cup frozen blueberries
- 1 packet (3.5 oz) frozen acai puree
- 1 banana
- 1 cup unsweetened almond milk
- 1 tbsp chia seeds
- 1 tbsp honey (optional)
- 1/2 cup ice cubes

### Directions

1. Add the frozen blueberries, acai puree, and banana to the blender.
2. Pour in the almond milk and add the chia seeds.
3. If desired, add honey for sweetness.
4. Add the ice cubes and blend on high until smooth and creamy.
5. Pour into glasses and serve immediately.

### Nutritional Information

Calories: 180, Protein: 3g, Carbohydrates: 38g, Fat: 4g, Fiber: 8g, Cholesterol: 0mg, Sodium: 60mg, Potassium: 450mg

# WARM LEMON & CAYENNE DETOX WATER

**Servings 2 | Prep: 5 min | Cook: 5 min**

This invigorating detox water combines the zesty freshness of lemon with a hint of cayenne heat, perfect for jumpstarting your metabolism and cleansing your system.

### Equipment

Small saucepan, Citrus juicer, Spoon

### Ingredients

- 2 cups water
- 1 lemon, juiced (about 2 oz)
- 1/4 tsp cayenne pepper
- 1 tbsp honey (optional)

### Directions

1. Heat the water in a small saucepan over medium heat until warm but not boiling.
2. Remove from heat and add the freshly squeezed lemon juice.
3. Stir in the cayenne pepper and honey, if using, until fully dissolved.
4. Pour into mugs and serve warm.

### Nutritional Information

Calories: 25, Protein: 0g, Carbohydrates: 7g, Fat: 0g, Fiber: 1g, Cholesterol: 0mg, Sodium: 1mg, Potassium: 80mg

# GINGER & PINEAPPLE DIGESTIVE TONIC

**Servings 4 | Prep: 10 min | Cook: 0 min**

This refreshing tonic combines the zesty kick of ginger with the tropical sweetness of pineapple, creating a delightful drink that aids digestion and invigorates the senses.

### Equipment

Blender, Fine Mesh Strainer, Measuring Cups

### Ingredients

- 2 cups fresh pineapple chunks
- 1 oz fresh ginger, peeled and sliced
- 2 cups coconut water
- 1 tbsp fresh lime juice
- 1 tsp honey (optional)

### Directions

1. Add pineapple chunks, ginger slices, and coconut water to the blender.
2. Blend on high until smooth and well combined.
3. Strain the mixture through a fine mesh strainer into a pitcher to remove pulp.
4. Stir in fresh lime juice and honey, if using, until well mixed.
5. Serve chilled or over ice for a refreshing experience.

### Nutritional Information

Calories: 60, Protein: 0.5g, Carbohydrates: 15g, Fat: 0g, Fiber: 1g, Cholesterol: 0mg, Sodium: 10mg, Potassium: 180mg

# HONEY-LAVENDER SLEEP TEA

**Servings 2 | Prep: 5 min | Cook: 10 min**

This soothing tea combines the calming properties of lavender with the natural sweetness of honey, perfect for unwinding before bedtime.

### Equipment

Small Saucepan, Fine Mesh Strainer, Teacups

### Ingredients

- 2 cups water
- 1 tbsp dried lavender flowers
- 1 tbsp honey
- 1 tsp chamomile flowers
- 1 tsp lemon juice

### Directions

1. Bring water to a gentle boil in a small saucepan.
2. Add dried lavender and chamomile flowers to the boiling water.
3. Reduce heat and let the mixture simmer for 5 minutes.
4. Remove from heat and strain the tea into teacups using a fine mesh strainer.
5. Stir in honey and lemon juice until fully dissolved.
6. Serve warm and enjoy a peaceful night's sleep.

### Nutritional Information

Calories: 35, Protein: 0g, Carbohydrates: 9g, Fat: 0g, Fiber: 0g, Cholesterol: 0mg, Sodium: 2mg, Potassium: 10mg

## CINNAMON & ALMOND SPICED LATTE

**Servings 2 | Prep: 5 min | Cook: 5 min**

A warm and comforting latte with a hint of cinnamon and the nutty flavor of almond milk, perfect for a cozy morning or an afternoon pick-me-up.

### Equipment

Saucepan, Whisk, Mug

### Ingredients

- 2 cups unsweetened almond milk
- 1 tbsp ground cinnamon
- 1 tbsp pure maple syrup
- 1 tsp vanilla extract
- 2 shots (2 oz each) of espresso or strong brewed coffee
- 1 cinnamon stick (optional, for garnish)

### Directions

1. In a saucepan over medium heat, combine the almond milk, ground cinnamon, maple syrup, and vanilla extract.
2. Whisk continuously until the mixture is heated through and slightly frothy, about 3-4 minutes.
3. Prepare the espresso or strong brewed coffee and divide it between two mugs.
4. Pour the spiced almond milk mixture over the coffee in each mug, stirring gently to combine.
5. Garnish with a cinnamon stick if desired, and serve immediately.

### Nutritional Information

Calories: 90, Protein: 1g, Carbohydrates: 15g, Fat: 3g, Fiber: 2g, Cholesterol: 0mg, Sodium: 150mg, Potassium: 200mg

## FRESH WATERMELON & BASIL JUICE

**Servings 4 | Prep: 10 min | Cook: 0 min**

This refreshing juice combines the sweet juiciness of watermelon with the aromatic freshness of basil, making it a perfect thirst-quencher for hot days.

### Equipment

Blender, Fine Mesh Strainer, Pitcher

### Ingredients

- 4 cups watermelon, cubed
- 1/4 cup fresh basil leaves
- 1 tbsp lime juice
- 1 tbsp honey (optional)
- 1 cup cold water
- Ice cubes (optional)

### Directions

1. Combine watermelon cubes and basil leaves in a blender.
2. Add lime juice, honey, and cold water to the blender.
3. Blend on high until smooth.
4. Pour the mixture through a fine mesh strainer into a pitcher to remove pulp.
5. Serve over ice cubes if desired.

### Nutritional Information

Calories: 60, Protein: 1g, Carbohydrates: 15g, Fat: 0g, Fiber: 1g, Cholesterol: 0mg, Sodium: 2mg, Potassium: 170mg

# CARROT, ORANGE & GINGER WELLNESS JUICE

**Servings 2 | Prep: 10 min | Cook: 0 min**

This invigorating juice combines the sweetness of carrots, the tang of oranges, and the zing of ginger to boost your immune system and energize your day.

### Equipment

Juicer, Peeler, Knife

### Ingredients

- 4 medium carrots, peeled and chopped
- 2 large oranges, peeled and segmented
- 1-inch piece of fresh ginger, peeled
- 1 tbsp lemon juice
- 1 cup cold water

### Directions

1. Prepare all ingredients by peeling and chopping as necessary.
2. Feed the carrots, oranges, and ginger through the juicer.
3. Collect the juice in a pitcher and stir in the lemon juice and cold water.
4. Pour into glasses and serve immediately for maximum freshness.
5. Optionally, garnish with a slice of orange or a sprig of mint.

### Nutritional Information

Calories: 120, Protein: 2g, Carbohydrates: 30g, Fat: 0.5g, Fiber: 5g, Cholesterol: 0mg, Sodium: 20mg, Potassium: 600mg

# APPLE CIDER VINEGAR MORNING SHOT

**Servings 1 | Prep: 5 min | Cook: 0 min**

Kickstart your day with this invigorating apple cider vinegar morning shot. It's a quick and refreshing way to boost your metabolism and energize your body.

### Equipment

Small glass, Measuring spoons, Stirring spoon

### Ingredients

- 2 tbsp apple cider vinegar
- 1 tbsp fresh lemon juice
- 1 tsp raw honey
- 1/4 tsp ground cinnamon
- 1/2 cup warm water

### Directions

1. In a small glass, combine the apple cider vinegar and fresh lemon juice.
2. Add the raw honey and ground cinnamon to the mixture.
3. Pour in the warm water and stir well until the honey is fully dissolved.
4. Taste and adjust sweetness if necessary by adding a little more honey.
5. Drink immediately for the best effect.

### Nutritional Information

Calories: 30, Protein: 0g, Carbohydrates: 8g, Fat: 0g, Fiber: 0g, Cholesterol: 0 mg, Sodium: 1 mg, Potassium: 20 mg

# PEPPERMINT & LEMON HERBAL INFUSION

**Servings 4 | Prep: 5 min | Cook: 10 min**

This refreshing herbal infusion combines the soothing properties of peppermint with the zesty brightness of lemon, creating a perfect beverage for relaxation and rejuvenation.

### Equipment

Medium Saucepan, Strainer, Teapot or Pitcher

### Ingredients

- 4 cups water
- 1 oz fresh peppermint leaves
- 1 lemon, thinly sliced
- 1 tbsp honey (optional)
- 1 tsp fresh ginger, grated (optional)

### Directions

1. Bring the water to a gentle boil in a medium saucepan.
2. Add the peppermint leaves and lemon slices to the boiling water.
3. Reduce heat and let it simmer for 5 minutes.
4. Remove from heat and strain the infusion into a teapot or pitcher.
5. Stir in honey and ginger, if using, and let it cool slightly before serving.

### Nutritional Information

Calories: 15, Protein: 0g, Carbohydrates: 4g, Fat: 0g, Fiber: 1g, Cholesterol: 0mg, Sodium: 2mg, Potassium: 45mg

# CUCUMBER & MINT COOLING TONIC

**Servings 4 | Prep: 10 min | Cook: 0 min**

This refreshing tonic combines the crispness of cucumber with the invigorating aroma of mint, perfect for a revitalizing drink on a warm day.

### Equipment

Blender, Fine Mesh Strainer, Pitcher

### Ingredients

- 1 large cucumber, peeled and chopped
- 1/4 cup fresh mint leaves
- 2 tbsp honey
- 1/4 cup fresh lime juice
- 3 cups cold water
- Ice cubes, for serving

### Directions

1. Blend the cucumber and mint leaves in a blender until smooth.
2. Strain the mixture through a fine mesh strainer into a pitcher to remove pulp.
3. Stir in the honey and lime juice until well combined.
4. Add the cold water and mix thoroughly.
5. Serve over ice cubes in glasses.

### Nutritional Information

Calories: 45, Protein: 0g, Carbohydrates: 12g, Fat: 0g, Fiber: 1g, Cholesterol: 0mg, Sodium: 5mg, Potassium: 120mg

# ANTI-INFLAMMATORY GREEN JUICE

**Servings 2 | Prep: 10 min | Cook: 0 min**

This refreshing green juice is packed with anti-inflammatory ingredients, perfect for boosting your immune system and energizing your day.

### Equipment

Juicer, Knife, Cutting Board

### Ingredients

- 2 cups kale leaves, packed
- 1 cup cucumber, chopped
- 1 green apple, cored and chopped
- 1 lemon, peeled
- 1-inch piece of ginger, peeled
- 1/2 cup celery, chopped
- 1/2 cup water

### Directions

1. Wash all produce thoroughly under running water.
2. Chop the kale, cucumber, apple, lemon, ginger, and celery into pieces that will fit into your juicer.
3. Feed the chopped ingredients into the juicer, alternating between soft and hard produce for optimal juicing.
4. Add water to the juice and stir well to combine.
5. Pour the juice into glasses and serve immediately for maximum freshness.

### Nutritional Information

Calories: 90, Protein: 2g, Carbohydrates: 22g, Fat: 0.5g, Fiber: 4g, Cholesterol: 0mg, Sodium: 50mg, Potassium: 450mg

# POMEGRANATE & LIME SPARKLING DRINK

**Servings 4 | Prep: 10 min | Cook: 0 min**

This refreshing and vibrant drink combines the tangy sweetness of pomegranate with the zesty kick of lime, all enhanced by a sparkling finish. Perfect for a healthy and invigorating treat.

### Equipment

Mixing Bowl, Citrus Juicer, Pitcher

### Ingredients

- 1 cup pomegranate juice
- 1/4 cup freshly squeezed lime juice
- 2 cups sparkling water
- 2 tbsp honey or agave syrup
- Ice cubes, as needed
- Lime slices, for garnish
- Pomegranate seeds, for garnish

### Directions

1. In a mixing bowl, combine the pomegranate juice and lime juice.
2. Stir in the honey or agave syrup until fully dissolved.
3. Pour the mixture into a pitcher and add the sparkling water.
4. Fill glasses with ice cubes and pour the drink over the ice.
5. Garnish with lime slices and pomegranate seeds before serving.

### Nutritional Information

Calories: 60, Protein: 0g, Carbohydrates: 16g, Fat: 0g, Fiber: 0g, Cholesterol: 0mg, Sodium: 5mg, Potassium: 120mg

# Desserts & Treats

# NO-BAKE ALMOND BUTTER BROWNIES

**Servings 12 | Prep: 15 min | Cook: 0 min**

Indulge in these rich, fudgy brownies that require no baking. Made with wholesome ingredients, they are a perfect guilt-free treat.

### Equipment

Food Processor, Mixing Bowl, 8x8-inch Baking Dish

### Ingredients

- 1 cup Almond Butter
- 1 cup Medjool Dates, pitted
- 1/2 cup Unsweetened Cocoa Powder
- 1/4 cup Almond Flour
- 1/4 cup Maple Syrup
- 1 tsp Vanilla Extract
- 1/4 tsp Sea Salt

### Directions

1. Combine almond butter, dates, cocoa powder, almond flour, maple syrup, vanilla extract, and sea salt in a food processor.
2. Process until the mixture is smooth and well combined.
3. Press the mixture evenly into an 8x8-inch baking dish lined with parchment paper.
4. Refrigerate for at least 30 minutes to set.
5. Cut into squares and serve chilled.

### Nutritional Information

Calories: 180, Protein: 4g, Carbohydrates: 22g, Fat: 10g, Fiber: 4g, Cholesterol: 0mg, Sodium: 50mg, Potassium: 280mg

# CHIA SEED CHOCOLATE PUDDING

**Servings 4 | Prep: 10 min | Cook: 0 min**

Indulge in a creamy, chocolatey delight that's both nutritious and satisfying. This chia seed chocolate pudding is a perfect guilt-free treat for any time of the day.

### Equipment

Mixing Bowl, Whisk, Measuring Cups, Refrigerator

### Ingredients

- 1/2 cup chia seeds
- 2 cups unsweetened almond milk
- 1/4 cup unsweetened cocoa powder
- 1/4 cup maple syrup
- 1 tsp vanilla extract
- 1/8 tsp salt

### Directions

1. In a mixing bowl, whisk together the almond milk, cocoa powder, maple syrup, vanilla extract, and salt until well combined.
2. Stir in the chia seeds, ensuring they are evenly distributed.
3. Cover the bowl and refrigerate for at least 4 hours or overnight, allowing the chia seeds to absorb the liquid and thicken.
4. Stir the pudding before serving to ensure a smooth consistency.
5. Serve chilled, optionally topped with fresh berries or a sprinkle of nuts for added texture.

### Nutritional Information

Calories: 180, Protein: 5g, Carbohydrates: 28g, Fat: 7g, Fiber: 10g, Cholesterol: 0mg, Sodium: 80mg, Potassium: 180mg

# COCONUT & DARK CHOCOLATE BLISS BALLS

**Servings 12 | Prep: 15 min | Cook: 0 min**

Indulge in these rich and satisfying Coconut & Dark Chocolate Bliss Balls, a perfect treat for those craving something sweet yet healthy. Packed with wholesome ingredients, they are a guilt-free delight.

### Equipment

Food Processor, Mixing Bowl, Baking Sheet

### Ingredients

- 1 cup unsweetened shredded coconut
- 1 cup pitted Medjool dates
- 2 tbsp unsweetened cocoa powder
- 2 tbsp almond butter
- 1 tsp vanilla extract
- 1/4 cup dark chocolate chips
- 1/4 tsp sea salt

### Directions

1. In a food processor, combine the shredded coconut, dates, cocoa powder, almond butter, vanilla extract, and sea salt.
2. Pulse until the mixture is well combined and sticky.
3. Transfer the mixture to a mixing bowl and fold in the dark chocolate chips.
4. Roll the mixture into 1-inch balls and place them on a baking sheet.
5. Refrigerate for at least 30 minutes to set before serving.

### Nutritional Information

Calories: 120, Protein: 2g, Carbohydrates: 15g, Fat: 7g, Fiber: 3g, Cholesterol: 0mg, Sodium: 20mg, Potassium: 180mg

# APPLE CINNAMON BAKED OAT BARS

**Servings 8 | Prep: 15 min | Cook: 30 min**

These Apple Cinnamon Baked Oat Bars are a wholesome treat, combining the comforting flavors of apple and cinnamon in a nutritious, easy-to-make snack.

### Equipment

Mixing Bowl, Baking Dish, Oven

### Ingredients

- 2 cups rolled oats
- 1 cup unsweetened applesauce
- 1/2 cup almond milk
- 1/4 cup honey
- 1 tsp vanilla extract
- 1 tsp ground cinnamon
- 1/2 tsp baking powder
- 1/4 tsp salt
- 1/2 cup diced apples

### Directions

1. Preheat the oven to 350°F (175°C) and lightly grease a baking dish.
2. In a mixing bowl, combine rolled oats, applesauce, almond milk, honey, and vanilla extract.
3. Add ground cinnamon, baking powder, and salt to the mixture, stirring until well combined.
4. Fold in the diced apples, ensuring they are evenly distributed.
5. Pour the mixture into the prepared baking dish and spread evenly.
6. Bake for 30 minutes or until the edges are golden brown and the center is set.
7. Allow to cool before cutting into bars.

### Nutritional Information

Calories: 150, Protein: 3g, Carbohydrates: 30g, Fat: 2g, Fiber: 4g, Cholesterol: 0mg, Sodium: 100mg, Potassium: 150mg

## DATE & WALNUT ENERGY FUDGE

**Servings 12 | Prep: 15 min | Cook: 0 min**

This Date & Walnut Energy Fudge is a delightful, no-bake treat that combines the natural sweetness of dates with the rich, nutty flavor of walnuts. Perfect for a quick energy boost or a guilt-free dessert.

### Equipment

Food Processor, Mixing Bowl, 8x8-inch Baking Dish

### Ingredients

- 1 cup pitted Medjool dates
- 1 cup raw walnuts
- 2 tbsp unsweetened cocoa powder
- 1 tbsp coconut oil
- 1 tsp vanilla extract
- 1/4 tsp sea salt

### Directions

1. In a food processor, combine the pitted dates and walnuts. Pulse until the mixture is finely chopped and starts to clump together.
2. Add the cocoa powder, coconut oil, vanilla extract, and sea salt to the processor. Blend until the mixture is smooth and well combined.
3. Transfer the mixture to an 8x8-inch baking dish lined with parchment paper. Press it down evenly to form a compact layer.
4. Refrigerate for at least 1 hour to allow the fudge to set.
5. Once set, cut into 12 squares and serve. Store any leftovers in an airtight container in the refrigerator.

### Nutritional Information

Calories: 120, Protein: 2g, Carbohydrates: 15g, Fat: 7g, Fiber: 2g, Cholesterol: 0mg, Sodium: 30mg, Potassium: 180mg

## RAW CASHEW CHEESECAKE BITES

**Servings 12 | Prep: 20 min | Cook: 0 min**

These Raw Cashew Cheesecake Bites are a creamy, indulgent treat that satisfy your sweet tooth while staying true to clean eating principles. Made with wholesome ingredients, they are perfect for a guilt-free dessert.

### Equipment

Food Processor, Muffin Tin, Blender

### Ingredients

- 1 cup raw cashews (soaked for 4 hours)
- 1/2 cup pitted dates
- 1/2 cup almonds
- 1/4 cup coconut oil, melted
- 1/4 cup maple syrup
- 1/4 cup lemon juice
- 1 tsp vanilla extract
- Pinch of sea salt

### Directions

1. Blend almonds and dates in a food processor until a sticky dough forms. Press the mixture into the bottom of a muffin tin to form the crust.
2. Drain and rinse the soaked cashews.
3. In a blender, combine cashews, coconut oil, maple syrup, lemon juice, vanilla extract, and sea salt. Blend until smooth and creamy.
4. Spoon the cashew mixture over the crust in the muffin tin, smoothing the tops with a spatula.
5. Freeze for at least 2 hours or until set.
6. Remove from the freezer and let sit for a few minutes before serving.

### Nutritional Information

Calories: 180, Protein: 4g, Carbohydrates: 16g, Fat: 12g, Fiber: 2g, Cholesterol: 0mg, Sodium: 10mg, Potassium: 150mg

# BANANA PEANUT BUTTER ICE CREAM

**Servings 4 | Prep: 10 min | Cook: 0 min**

Indulge in a creamy, guilt-free treat with this Banana Peanut Butter Ice Cream. It's a perfect blend of natural sweetness and nutty richness, ideal for satisfying your dessert cravings while staying true to clean eating principles.

### Equipment

Blender, Freezer-safe Container, Spatula

### Ingredients

- 4 ripe bananas, sliced and frozen
- 1/4 cup natural peanut butter
- 1/2 tsp vanilla extract
- 1/4 cup unsweetened almond milk
- 1 tbsp honey (optional)

### Directions

1. Place the frozen banana slices in a blender.
2. Add peanut butter, vanilla extract, and almond milk.
3. Blend until smooth and creamy, scraping down the sides as needed.
4. Taste and add honey if additional sweetness is desired, then blend again.
5. Transfer the mixture to a freezer-safe container and freeze for at least 2 hours.
6. Scoop and serve immediately for a soft-serve texture or freeze longer for a firmer consistency.

### Nutritional Information

Calories: 210, Protein: 4g, Carbohydrates: 36g, Fat: 8g, Fiber: 4g, Cholesterol: 0mg, Sodium: 40mg, Potassium: 550mg

# LEMON COCONUT MACAROONS

**Servings 12 | Prep: 15 min | Cook: 20 min**

These Lemon Coconut Macaroons are a delightful blend of zesty lemon and sweet coconut, offering a refreshing twist on a classic treat. Perfect for a guilt-free indulgence.

### Equipment

Mixing Bowl, Baking Sheet, Parchment Paper

### Ingredients

- 2 cups unsweetened shredded coconut
- 1/2 cup almond flour
- 1/2 cup pure maple syrup
- 1 tsp vanilla extract
- 1 tbsp lemon zest
- 2 tbsp fresh lemon juice
- 1/4 tsp sea salt

### Directions

1. Preheat the oven to 325°F (163°C) and line a baking sheet with parchment paper.
2. In a mixing bowl, combine shredded coconut, almond flour, and sea salt.
3. Add maple syrup, vanilla extract, lemon zest, and lemon juice to the dry ingredients. Mix until well combined.
4. Scoop tablespoon-sized amounts of the mixture and form into small mounds on the prepared baking sheet.
5. Bake for 18-20 minutes or until the edges are golden brown.
6. Allow to cool on the baking sheet for 5 minutes before transferring to a wire rack to cool completely.

### Nutritional Information

Calories: 120, Protein: 1g, Carbohydrates: 12g, Fat: 8g, Fiber: 2g, Cholesterol: 0mg, Sodium: 30mg, Potassium: 60mg

## MAPLE & PECAN BAKED PEARS

**Servings 4 | Prep: 10 min | Cook: 25 min**

These Maple & Pecan Baked Pears are a delightful, warm dessert that combines the natural sweetness of pears with the rich flavors of maple syrup and crunchy pecans. Perfect for a cozy evening treat.

### Equipment

Baking Dish, Mixing Bowl, Spoon

### Ingredients

- 2 ripe pears, halved and cored
- 1/4 cup pure maple syrup
- 1/4 cup chopped pecans
- 1/2 tsp ground cinnamon
- 1/4 tsp vanilla extract
- 1 tbsp unsalted butter, melted

### Directions

1. Preheat the oven to 350°F (175°C).
2. Arrange the pear halves in a baking dish, cut side up.
3. In a mixing bowl, combine maple syrup, chopped pecans, cinnamon, vanilla extract, and melted butter.
4. Spoon the mixture over the pears, ensuring even coverage.
5. Bake for 25 minutes, or until the pears are tender and caramelized.
6. Serve warm, optionally with a dollop of Greek yogurt or a sprinkle of extra pecans.

### Nutritional Information

Calories: 180, Protein: 1g, Carbohydrates: 28g, Fat: 8g, Fiber: 4g, Cholesterol: 5mg, Sodium: 5mg, Potassium: 210mg

## HOMEMADE RASPBERRY CHIA JAM

**Servings 8 | Prep: 5 min | Cook: 10 min**

This Homemade Raspberry Chia Jam is a delightful, naturally sweetened spread perfect for toast, yogurt, or desserts. It's packed with fresh raspberry flavor and the nutritional benefits of chia seeds.

### Equipment

Medium Saucepan, Wooden Spoon, Mason Jar

### Ingredients

- 2 cups fresh raspberries
- 2 tbsp chia seeds
- 2 tbsp honey (or maple syrup for a vegan option)
- 1 tsp vanilla extract
- 1 tbsp lemon juice

### Directions

1. In a medium saucepan, combine raspberries and honey over medium heat. Stir occasionally until the raspberries break down and become syrupy, about 5 minutes.
2. Remove from heat and stir in chia seeds, vanilla extract, and lemon juice. Mix well to combine.
3. Let the mixture sit for 5 minutes to allow the chia seeds to thicken the jam.
4. Transfer the jam to a mason jar and let it cool to room temperature.
5. Store in the refrigerator for up to two weeks.

### Nutritional Information

Calories: 40, Protein: 1g, Carbohydrates: 8g, Fat: 1g, Fiber: 3g, Cholesterol: 0mg, Sodium: 1mg, Potassium: 60mg

# DARK CHOCOLATE AVOCADO MOUSSE

**Servings 4 | Prep: 10 min | Cook: 0 min**

Indulge in a rich and creamy dessert that combines the decadence of dark chocolate with the health benefits of avocado. This mousse is a guilt-free treat that satisfies your sweet tooth while keeping it clean and wholesome.

### Equipment

Blender, Mixing Bowl, Spatula

### Ingredients

- 2 ripe avocados, peeled and pitted
- 1/2 cup unsweetened cocoa powder
- 1/4 cup pure maple syrup
- 1/4 cup almond milk
- 1 tsp vanilla extract
- 1/4 tsp sea salt
- 2 oz dark chocolate, melted

### Directions

1. In a blender, combine the avocados, cocoa powder, maple syrup, almond milk, vanilla extract, and sea salt.
2. Blend until smooth and creamy, scraping down the sides as needed.
3. Add the melted dark chocolate to the blender and blend again until fully incorporated.
4. Taste and adjust sweetness if necessary by adding more maple syrup.
5. Transfer the mousse to a mixing bowl and chill in the refrigerator for at least 30 minutes before serving.
6. Serve chilled, optionally garnished with fresh berries or a sprinkle of cocoa nibs.

### Nutritional Information

Calories: 250, Protein: 4g, Carbohydrates: 28g, Fat: 17g, Fiber: 8g, Cholesterol: 0mg, Sodium: 75mg, Potassium: 550mg

# OATMEAL & BLUEBERRY MUFFINS

**Servings 12 | Prep: 15 min | Cook: 20 min**

These Oatmeal & Blueberry Muffins are a delightful treat, combining the wholesome goodness of oats with the juicy burst of blueberries. Perfect for a clean eating lifestyle, they are both nourishing and delicious.

### Equipment

Muffin Tin, Mixing Bowl, Whisk

### Ingredients

- 1 cup Rolled Oats
- 1 cup Whole Wheat Flour
- 1/2 cup Unsweetened Almond Milk
- 1/3 cup Honey
- 1/4 cup Coconut Oil, melted
- 1 tsp Baking Powder
- 1/2 tsp Baking Soda
- 1/2 tsp Cinnamon
- 1/4 tsp Salt
- 1 cup Fresh Blueberries
- 1 large Egg

### Directions

1. Preheat the oven to 350°F and line a muffin tin with paper liners.
2. In a mixing bowl, combine rolled oats, whole wheat flour, baking powder, baking soda, cinnamon, and salt.
3. In another bowl, whisk together almond milk, honey, melted coconut oil, and egg until well combined.
4. Pour the wet ingredients into the dry ingredients and stir until just combined. Gently fold in the blueberries.
5. Divide the batter evenly among the muffin cups and bake for 18-20 minutes, or until a toothpick inserted into the center comes out clean.
6. Allow muffins to cool in the tin for 5 minutes before transferring to a wire rack to cool completely.

### Nutritional Information

Calories: 150, Protein: 3g, Carbohydrates: 25g, Fat: 5g, Fiber: 3g, Cholesterol: 15mg, Sodium: 120mg, Potassium: 100mg

## SWEET POTATO & CACAO FUDGE

**Servings 12 | Prep: 15 min | Cook: 30 min**

Indulge in this rich and creamy fudge made with wholesome ingredients. The natural sweetness of sweet potatoes pairs perfectly with the deep flavor of cacao, creating a guilt-free treat.

### Equipment

Blender, Baking Dish, Saucepan

### Ingredients

- 1 cup mashed sweet potatoes (about 2 medium sweet potatoes)
- 1/2 cup cacao powder
- 1/4 cup almond butter
- 1/4 cup pure maple syrup
- 1 tsp vanilla extract
- 1/4 tsp sea salt
- 1/4 cup chopped walnuts (optional)

### Directions

1. Preheat the oven to 350°F. Pierce sweet potatoes with a fork and bake for 30 minutes or until tender. Let cool, then peel and mash.
2. In a saucepan over low heat, combine mashed sweet potatoes, almond butter, maple syrup, vanilla extract, and sea salt. Stir until smooth.
3. Remove from heat and mix in cacao powder until fully incorporated.
4. Pour the mixture into a lined baking dish, spreading evenly. Sprinkle chopped walnuts on top if using.
5. Refrigerate for at least 2 hours or until set. Cut into squares and serve.

### Nutritional Information

Calories: 110, Protein: 2g, Carbohydrates: 16g, Fat: 5g, Fiber: 3g, Cholesterol: 0mg, Sodium: 45mg, Potassium: 200mg

## RAW CARROT CAKE BITES

**Servings 12 | Prep: 15 min | Cook: 0 min**

These Raw Carrot Cake Bites are a delightful, guilt-free treat that captures the essence of a classic carrot cake in a healthy, bite-sized form. Perfect for satisfying your sweet tooth while staying true to clean eating principles.

### Equipment

Food Processor, Mixing Bowl, Baking Sheet

### Ingredients

- 1 cup grated carrots
- 1 cup pitted dates
- 1 cup raw walnuts
- 1/2 cup unsweetened shredded coconut
- 1 tsp ground cinnamon
- 1/2 tsp ground nutmeg
- 1/4 tsp sea salt
- 1 tsp vanilla extract

### Directions

1. In a food processor, combine the walnuts and dates. Pulse until a sticky mixture forms.
2. Add the grated carrots, shredded coconut, cinnamon, nutmeg, sea salt, and vanilla extract to the mixture. Pulse until well combined.
3. Scoop out tablespoon-sized amounts of the mixture and roll them into balls.
4. Place the carrot cake bites on a baking sheet lined with parchment paper.
5. Refrigerate for at least 30 minutes to firm up before serving.

### Nutritional Information

Calories: 90, Protein: 2g, Carbohydrates: 12g, Fat: 5g, Fiber: 2g, Cholesterol: 0mg, Sodium: 20mg, Potassium: 150mg

# BAKED APPLE & CINNAMON CRISP

**Servings 6 | Prep: 15 min | Cook: 30 min**

This delightful Baked Apple & Cinnamon Crisp combines the natural sweetness of apples with the warm, comforting flavors of cinnamon and oats. It's a perfect clean-eating dessert that satisfies your sweet tooth without the guilt.

### Equipment

Baking Dish, Mixing Bowl, Oven

### Ingredients

- 4 cups thinly sliced apples (about 4 medium apples)
- 1 tsp ground cinnamon
- 1 tbsp lemon juice
- 1/2 cup rolled oats
- 1/4 cup almond flour
- 1/4 cup chopped walnuts
- 3 tbsp maple syrup
- 2 tbsp coconut oil, melted
- 1/4 tsp sea salt

### Directions

1. Preheat the oven to 350°F (175°C).
2. In a mixing bowl, combine the sliced apples, lemon juice, and 1/2 tsp of cinnamon. Toss to coat the apples evenly.
3. Spread the apple mixture evenly in the baking dish.
4. In the same mixing bowl, combine the oats, almond flour, walnuts, remaining cinnamon, maple syrup, melted coconut oil, and sea salt. Mix until crumbly.
5. Sprinkle the oat mixture evenly over the apples.
6. Bake in the preheated oven for 30 minutes, or until the topping is golden brown and the apples are tender.
7. Allow to cool slightly before serving. Enjoy warm or at room temperature.

### Nutritional Information

Calories: 210, Protein: 3g, Carbohydrates: 30g, Fat: 10g, Fiber: 4g, Cholesterol: 0mg, Sodium: 50mg, Potassium: 220mg

# CHOCOLATE-DIPPED BANANA BITES

**Servings 12 | Prep: 15 min | Cook: 0 min**

Indulge in these delightful Chocolate-Dipped Banana Bites, a perfect blend of creamy banana and rich dark chocolate, offering a guilt-free treat for any occasion.

### Equipment

Baking Sheet, Parchment Paper, Microwave-Safe Bowl

### Ingredients

- 3 medium bananas, peeled and sliced into 1-inch pieces
- 8 oz dark chocolate chips
- 2 tbsp unsweetened shredded coconut
- 2 tbsp chopped nuts (such as almonds or walnuts)

### Directions

1. Line a baking sheet with parchment paper.
2. Melt the dark chocolate chips in a microwave-safe bowl in 30-second intervals, stirring in between, until smooth.
3. Dip each banana slice halfway into the melted chocolate, allowing excess to drip off.
4. Place the dipped banana slices onto the prepared baking sheet.
5. Sprinkle with shredded coconut and chopped nuts while the chocolate is still wet.
6. Freeze for at least 1 hour or until the chocolate is set.
7. Serve immediately or store in an airtight container in the freezer.

### Nutritional Information

Calories: 95, Protein: 1g, Carbohydrates: 15g, Fat: 5g, Fiber: 2g, Cholesterol: 0mg, Sodium: 2mg, Potassium: 210mg

# STRAWBERRY COCONUT YOGURT BARK

**Servings 8 | Prep: 10 min | Cook: 0 min**

This refreshing and creamy strawberry coconut yogurt bark is a delightful treat that combines the natural sweetness of strawberries with the creamy texture of yogurt and a hint of coconut. Perfect for a healthy snack or a light dessert.

### Equipment

Baking Sheet, Parchment Paper, Mixing Bowl

### Ingredients

- 2 cups plain Greek yogurt
- 2 tbsp honey
- 1 tsp vanilla extract
- 1 cup strawberries, sliced
- 1/4 cup unsweetened shredded coconut

### Directions

1. Line a baking sheet with parchment paper.
2. In a mixing bowl, combine the Greek yogurt, honey, and vanilla extract until smooth.
3. Spread the yogurt mixture evenly onto the prepared baking sheet.
4. Scatter the sliced strawberries and shredded coconut over the yogurt.
5. Freeze for at least 3 hours or until completely firm.
6. Break into pieces and serve immediately or store in the freezer for later.

### Nutritional Information

Calories: 90, Protein: 5g, Carbohydrates: 12g, Fat: 3g, Fiber: 1g, Cholesterol: 5mg, Sodium: 30mg, Potassium: 150mg

# PUMPKIN SPICE ENERGY BALLS

**Servings 12 | Prep: 15 min | Cook: 0 min**

These Pumpkin Spice Energy Balls are a delightful blend of fall flavors, perfect for a quick snack or a healthy treat. Packed with nutrients and natural sweetness, they offer a guilt-free indulgence.

### Equipment

Food Processor, Mixing Bowl, Measuring Cups and Spoons

### Ingredients

- 1 cup rolled oats
- 1/2 cup canned pumpkin puree
- 1/2 cup almond butter
- 1/4 cup honey
- 1 tsp pumpkin pie spice
- 1/2 tsp vanilla extract
- 1/4 cup mini dark chocolate chips (optional)

### Directions

1. In a food processor, pulse the rolled oats until they reach a coarse flour-like consistency.
2. In a mixing bowl, combine the pumpkin puree, almond butter, honey, pumpkin pie spice, and vanilla extract. Mix until smooth.
3. Add the processed oats to the pumpkin mixture and stir until well combined.
4. Fold in the mini dark chocolate chips, if using.
5. Using your hands, roll the mixture into 1-inch balls.
6. Place the energy balls on a plate and refrigerate for at least 30 minutes to firm up.

### Nutritional Information

Calories: 110, Protein: 3g, Carbohydrates: 14g, Fat: 6g, Fiber: 2g, Cholesterol: 0mg, Sodium: 5mg, Potassium: 100mg

# MANGO & COCONUT SORBET

### Servings 4 | Prep: 10 min | Cook: 0 min

This refreshing Mango & Coconut Sorbet is a tropical delight, perfect for satisfying your sweet tooth while keeping it clean and healthy.

### Equipment

Blender, Freezer-safe container, Measuring cups

### Ingredients

- 2 cups ripe mango, diced
- 1 cup coconut milk
- 2 tbsp honey or maple syrup
- 1 tbsp lime juice
- 1 tsp vanilla extract

### Directions

1. Combine the diced mango, coconut milk, honey, lime juice, and vanilla extract in a blender.
2. Blend until smooth and creamy.
3. Pour the mixture into a freezer-safe container.
4. Freeze for at least 4 hours or until firm.
5. Scoop and serve immediately for a refreshing treat.

### Nutritional Information

Calories: 150, Protein: 1g, Carbohydrates: 28g, Fat: 6g, Fiber: 2g, Cholesterol: 0mg, Sodium: 15mg, Potassium: 250mg

# MATCHA & PISTACHIO PROTEIN BALLS

### Servings 12 | Prep: 15 min | Cook: 0 min

These Matcha & Pistachio Protein Balls are a delightful blend of earthy matcha and crunchy pistachios, perfect for a quick energy boost or a healthy treat.

### Equipment

Food Processor, Mixing Bowl, Measuring Cups

### Ingredients

- 1 cup raw pistachios
- 1 cup pitted Medjool dates
- 2 tbsp matcha powder
- 1/4 cup almond butter
- 1 tbsp chia seeds
- 1 tsp vanilla extract
- 1/4 tsp sea salt

### Directions

1. In a food processor, pulse the pistachios until finely ground.
2. Add the dates, matcha powder, almond butter, chia seeds, vanilla extract, and sea salt to the processor.
3. Blend until the mixture is well combined and forms a sticky dough.
4. Roll the mixture into 1-inch balls using your hands.
5. Place the balls on a plate and refrigerate for at least 30 minutes to set.

### Nutritional Information

Calories: 120, Protein: 3g, Carbohydrates: 15g, Fat: 6g, Fiber: 3g, Cholesterol: 0mg, Sodium: 30mg, Potassium: 180mg

# HONEY & ALMOND BAKED PEACHES

**Servings 4 | Prep: 10 min | Cook: 20 min**

Juicy peaches are transformed into a delightful dessert with a touch of honey and the crunch of almonds, offering a perfect balance of sweetness and texture.

### Equipment

Baking Dish, Mixing Bowl, Oven

### Ingredients

- 4 ripe peaches, halved and pitted
- 2 tbsp honey
- 1/4 cup sliced almonds
- 1 tsp ground cinnamon
- 1 tbsp coconut oil, melted

### Directions

1. Preheat the oven to 350°F (175°C).
2. Arrange the peach halves in a baking dish, cut side up.
3. Drizzle each peach half with honey and sprinkle with cinnamon.
4. Scatter sliced almonds over the peaches and drizzle with melted coconut oil.
5. Bake for 20 minutes, or until peaches are tender and almonds are golden.
6. Serve warm, optionally with a dollop of Greek yogurt or a scoop of vanilla ice cream.

### Nutritional Information

Calories: 150, Protein: 2g, Carbohydrates: 20g, Fat: 7g, Fiber: 3g, Cholesterol: 0mg, Sodium: 0mg, Potassium: 285mg

# CACAO NIB & DATE BROWNIES

**Servings 12 | Prep: 15 min | Cook: 25 min**

Indulge in these rich and fudgy brownies, naturally sweetened with dates and enhanced with the crunch of cacao nibs. A perfect guilt-free treat for any chocolate lover.

### Equipment

Food Processor, Mixing Bowl, Baking Pan (8x8 inches)

### Ingredients

- 1 cup pitted Medjool dates
- 1/2 cup unsweetened applesauce
- 1/4 cup almond butter
- 1/2 cup cacao powder
- 1/4 cup cacao nibs
- 1/2 tsp baking soda
- 1/4 tsp sea salt
- 1 tsp vanilla extract

### Directions

1. Preheat the oven to 350°F (175°C) and line the baking pan with parchment paper.
2. In a food processor, blend the dates until they form a paste.
3. Add applesauce, almond butter, cacao powder, baking soda, sea salt, and vanilla extract to the date paste. Blend until smooth.
4. Stir in the cacao nibs by hand.
5. Pour the batter into the prepared baking pan and spread evenly.
6. Bake for 25 minutes or until a toothpick inserted in the center comes out clean.
7. Allow to cool before slicing into squares.

### Nutritional Information

Calories: 120, Protein: 2g, Carbohydrates: 20g, Fat: 5g, Fiber: 4g, Cholesterol: 0mg, Sodium: 50mg, Potassium: 220mg

# HAZELNUT & FIG RAW BARS

**Servings 12 | Prep: 15 min | Cook: 0 min**

These Hazelnut & Fig Raw Bars are a delightful blend of natural sweetness and nutty richness, perfect for a clean eating treat that satisfies your sweet tooth without any guilt.

### Equipment

Food Processor, 8x8-inch Baking Dish, Parchment Paper

### Ingredients

- 1 cup raw hazelnuts
- 1 cup dried figs, stems removed
- 1 cup Medjool dates, pitted
- 1/2 cup unsweetened shredded coconut
- 1 tbsp chia seeds
- 1 tsp vanilla extract
- 1/4 tsp sea salt

### Directions

1. Line an 8x8-inch baking dish with parchment paper, leaving some overhang for easy removal.
2. In a food processor, pulse the hazelnuts until finely chopped.
3. Add figs, dates, shredded coconut, chia seeds, vanilla extract, and sea salt to the processor. Blend until the mixture is sticky and holds together when pressed.
4. Transfer the mixture to the prepared baking dish. Press firmly and evenly into the dish using your hands or a spatula.
5. Refrigerate for at least 1 hour to set. Once firm, lift out of the dish using the parchment overhang and cut into bars.

### Nutritional Information

Calories: 180, Protein: 3g, Carbohydrates: 25g, Fat: 9g, Fiber: 4g, Cholesterol: 0mg, Sodium: 30mg, Potassium: 250mg

# GINGER-SPICED BAKED APPLES

**Servings 4 | Prep: 10 min | Cook: 30 min**

These Ginger-Spiced Baked Apples are a warm, comforting treat that combines the natural sweetness of apples with the zing of ginger and cinnamon, perfect for a cozy dessert.

### Equipment

Baking Dish, Mixing Bowl, Knife

### Ingredients

- 4 medium apples, cored
- 1/4 cup rolled oats
- 2 tbsp chopped walnuts
- 2 tbsp raisins
- 2 tbsp honey
- 1 tsp ground ginger
- 1 tsp ground cinnamon
- 1/4 cup water

### Directions

1. Preheat the oven to 350°F (175°C).
2. In a mixing bowl, combine oats, walnuts, raisins, honey, ginger, and cinnamon.
3. Stuff each cored apple with the oat mixture, pressing down gently.
4. Place the stuffed apples in a baking dish and pour water into the bottom of the dish.
5. Bake for 30 minutes, or until apples are tender.
6. Let cool slightly before serving.

### Nutritional Information

Calories: 180, Protein: 2g, Carbohydrates: 40g, Fat: 4g, Fiber: 5g, Cholesterol: 0mg, Sodium: 5mg, Potassium: 220mg

# CRANBERRY & WALNUT OAT COOKIES

**Servings 12 | Prep: 15 min | Cook: 12 min**

These wholesome cookies combine the tartness of cranberries with the crunch of walnuts, all nestled in a hearty oat base. Perfect for a guilt-free treat!

### Equipment

Mixing Bowl, Baking Sheet, Parchment Paper

### Ingredients

- 1 cup rolled oats
- 1/2 cup whole wheat flour
- 1/2 tsp baking soda
- 1/4 tsp salt
- 1/3 cup coconut oil, melted
- 1/3 cup honey
- 1 tsp vanilla extract
- 1/2 cup dried cranberries
- 1/2 cup chopped walnuts

### Directions

1. Preheat the oven to 350°F (175°C) and line a baking sheet with parchment paper.
2. In a mixing bowl, combine oats, flour, baking soda, and salt.
3. In a separate bowl, whisk together melted coconut oil, honey, and vanilla extract.
4. Pour the wet ingredients into the dry ingredients and mix until combined. Fold in cranberries and walnuts.
5. Drop tablespoon-sized amounts of dough onto the prepared baking sheet, spacing them about 2 inches apart.
6. Bake for 10-12 minutes, or until the edges are golden brown. Let cool on a wire rack.

### Nutritional Information

Calories: 150, Protein: 2g, Carbohydrates: 20g, Fat: 8g, Fiber: 2g, Cholesterol: 0mg, Sodium: 60mg, Potassium: 80mg

# VANILLA & CHIA YOGURT PARFAITS

**Servings 4 | Prep: 10 min | Cook: 0 min**

Indulge in a creamy, nutrient-packed parfait that combines the richness of vanilla yogurt with the crunch of chia seeds and fresh berries. Perfect for a healthy dessert or a refreshing breakfast treat.

### Equipment

Mixing Bowl, Whisk, Parfait Glasses

### Ingredients

- 2 cups vanilla Greek yogurt
- 2 tablespoons chia seeds
- 1 cup mixed fresh berries (such as strawberries, blueberries, and raspberries)
- 1 tablespoon honey
- 1 teaspoon vanilla extract
- 1/4 cup granola

### Directions

1. In a mixing bowl, combine the vanilla Greek yogurt, chia seeds, honey, and vanilla extract. Whisk until well blended.
2. Let the mixture sit for about 5 minutes to allow the chia seeds to expand slightly.
3. Layer the yogurt mixture into parfait glasses, alternating with layers of mixed berries.
4. Top each parfait with a sprinkle of granola for added crunch.
5. Serve immediately or refrigerate for up to 2 hours for a chilled treat.

### Nutritional Information

Calories: 180, Protein: 8g, Carbohydrates: 28g, Fat: 4g, Fiber: 5g, Cholesterol: 5mg, Sodium: 55mg, Potassium: 250mg

Printed in Dunstable, United Kingdom